the intentional networker

Patti DeNucci

Attracting Powerful Relationships, Referrals & Results In Business

The Intentional Networker: Attracting powerful relationships, referrals & results in business
By Patti DeNucci
Rosewall Press

Published by Rosewall Press, Austin, TX

Editor: Kim Pearson, www.primary-sources.com
Index: Nancy Humphreys, www.wordmapsindexing.com
Cover and Interior design: Bella Guzmán, www.highwirecreative.com
Cover image: Blank business (visit) card by ouh_desire, 2011. Used under license from Shutterstock.com

Library of Congress Control Number: 2011907118

DeNucci, Patti
The intentional networker: attracting powerful relationships, referrals & results in business / Patti DeNucci. – 1st ed.

ISBN: 978-0-9835461-0-8

Includes index.

Bibliographical references and resources can be found at www.theintentionalnetworker.com/resources.

Disclaimer: The names in some of the stories have been changed in this book at author's discretion or the participants' request.

ATTENTION CORPORATIONS, UNIVERSITIES, COLLEGES AND PROFESSIONAL ORGANIZATIONS: Quantity discounts are available on bulk purchases of this book for large groups, sales promotions, as gifts, or for educational purposes. Special books or book excerpts can also be created to fit specific needs. For information, please contact: Rosewall Press, 5114 Balcones Woods Dr., 307-430, Austin, TX 78759, 512-418-0527

*In memory of my loving and extraordinary
parents, Kenneth and Ersel Parks*

contents

foreword

BY SANDRA YANCEY

When I founded eWomenNetwork™ in 2000 and released my book *Relationship Networking: The Art of Turning Contacts into Connections* in 2006, one of my goals was to empower success-minded business women to use, honor, and sharpen their natural relationship-building instincts and talents to turn everyday contacts into powerful business and life connections. Today, my work continues as I lead this premier women's business network with 118 chapters around the globe, connecting more than 500,000 smart and savvy women from all over the world. My work is to do everything I can to inspire and encourage business women to embrace their talents and competencies to become even more successful, profitable, and powerful as they launch and grow their own enterprises and create positive changes in the world.

In her book *The Intentional Networker: Attracting Powerful Relationships, Referrals & Results in Business*, Patti DeNucci—a long-time eWomenNetwork member and advocate—offers her own important and unique perspective on the principles of authentic, relationship-driven connecting. Patti offers nine rich chapters filled with stories, secrets, techniques, and tips she has acquired in more than twenty years as an entrepreneur, prolific business matchmaker, intentional networker, and champion of purpose-driven entrepreneurs.

I first met Patti in 2002 when I interviewed her for the eWomenNetwork radio show on ABC. Shortly thereafter, she joined eWomenNetwork. Again in 2010 I had the distinct pleasure of interviewing her on a

Tele-Seminar with the eWomenNetwork Success Institute. During these exchanges, Patti offered great insights as she spoke of the high standards she knew she had to acquire, refine, and uphold throughout her career if she was to succeed and compete in the corporate and agency worlds, as an independent business communications expert, and especially in her work as a professional connector for her business referral firm, DeNucci & Co. These high standards include being more focused, deliberate, and discerning about which networking groups she joins, which events she attends, which connections and relationships she develops and nurtures, and which relationships are worthy of referrals. Whether the economic times are robust or challenging, Patti's principles work! She has proven that both wildly profitable and lean-and-mean times demand being intentional and selective. She knows that doing so prevents you from wasting valuable time and resources.

Since our initial exchanges, our relationship has blossomed. I am honored to consider Patti among my girlfriends! We share so many of the same values around the importance of gaining and growing great relationships – both personally and professionally. We never tire of sharing our most recently acquired news, stories, experiences, and epiphanies on the power of showing up; seeking, initiating, and building high quality connections with other likeminded business leaders; setting and raising our own standards; and reaching toward that next level of success and innovation in business. We have learned through firsthand experience, and from working with many other successful business people, that raising the bar and finding focus in our business connections are keys to earning respect, referrals, and results in business.

With this book, Patti is passing the torch and extending those keys of success to you. As you read, I believe you'll find her to be direct, but also gracious and encouraging as she shares experiences, secrets, and stories she has collected and put to use during a career of building business relationships. Undoubtedly, you will garner great insights and strategies that you can immediately apply in your own life.

Here's to raising your own connections bar in business as you build your knowledge of the power of being more intentional, authentic, values-centered, and successful as a networker, referral builder, and savvy, selective businessperson. And here's to my dear friend, Patti DeNucci, for giving us the gift of her wisdom to make it so!

Sandra Yancey
Founder & CEO
eWomenNetwork, Inc.

introduction

All my life, whether I knew it or not, I was preparing to be a networking and referral expert. I grew up watching and admiring my dad, a WWII veteran and auto dealer in a small town in Northern Minnesota. Dad was gregarious by nature, friendly, and courteous with everyone: friends, neighbors, customers, employees, and even his competitors in nearby towns. People in turn were drawn to him, which helped him build and run a successful business that supported our family of six comfortably for more than four decades. Then there was Mom, a classy, cordial, and steady woman; the ninth child of British immigrants. She was kind and gracious to *everyone*, even some of our most questionable friends. Yet Mom enjoyed her solitude, liked to get things done, and was choosy about how and with whom she spent her time. She often suggested that we consider doing the same.

Growing up I felt the influence of Dad, the extroverted entrepreneur and relationship builder, and Mom, the gracious, hardworking, and selective homebody and introvert. Not surprisingly, personality tests reveal that I fall on the cusp of these diverse personalities. I love being out among good people and connecting them to each other. Yet I also relish my time alone to write, work on projects, think, and create.

The influence of my parents provided the earliest examples and lessons of a lifetime on the art and power of purposeful relationships, mindful connecting, intention, and balance.

After getting my college degree, I spent two years in a corporate communications job I hated and nearly seven years in a marketing communications agency job I loved. In 1989, I launched my own freelance and consulting practice. If there was ever a time to put all my networking and people skills to work, this was it. I began writing letters and making calls to everyone I knew, had done business with – and *still liked*. I let them know I was on my own, open for business, eager to reconnect with them, and put my talents, skills, and experience to work to serve them.

Some of my clients came from existing contacts; others were the result of networking I did with the Association for Women in Communications (AWC), the Austin Writers League (now the Writers League of Texas), and other organizations and gatherings. As much as I liked AWC and AWL, I also yearned for a networking group that brought together business-minded freelancers like me. Seeing there was no such group in my city, I created one. I called it the First Tuesday Freelancers Group. We met once a month over brown bag lunches to discuss a variety of topics: how to find more clients, how to better serve the ones we had, and how to tactfully ditch the ones we didn't like. I loved this group, not only because of what I got out of it, but mostly because it fed my passions for connecting and for leading other freelancers and entrepreneurs toward greater learning, professional growth, and success. It is one of my proudest accomplishments. More than twenty years later the group is still thriving. Today it has a better name, Freelance Austin, and has been taken under the wing of our local professional chapter of AWC.

With all the strategic networking I was doing for my business, something wonderful happened: I attracted more business than I could handle. I began to refer the overflow to colleagues, but only the ones I knew and trusted *implicitly* to serve the clients well. If I couldn't serve the prospects who came to me, I would help them find someone just as good or *better*. The thanks I received in return was both satisfying and empowering. My phone kept on ringing, not only with more business, but with more "Who do you know?" questions.

In 2001, my biggest client was snapped up by a competitor with plenty of in-house communications help; I was no longer needed. At that point I opened myself up to doing something new. A business consultant who knew me well suggested I create a referral business. "You'd be perfect for this," she said. "You clearly have many powerful and talented people in your database, you know how to attract business, and you know how to make good referrals. You're already doing this. Why not make it your business?" We mapped out a business model and DeNucci & Co. was born.

My work turned from serving my own freelance clients to strategically and selectively connecting businesses to the capable freelancers, consultants, and other resources they needed for their marketing communications projects. I realized that it was more critical than ever to do my matchmaking well. After all, who I referred and how the connection worked out had a direct and profound impact on all involved. It also reflected on my brand and reputation, and impacted my chances of earning more business.

Being this particular in my referrals likewise demanded that I become more particular, focused, and intentional in my networking. I wanted to be around the types of people I enjoyed, found energizing and inspiring, and felt good connecting. Networking more purposefully helped me hone in on these people. The result was more business, higher quality matchmaking, and a lot less time out and about, randomly exchanging business cards. I made more money and had a lot more fun as well.

Over the last ten years, publications, companies, and associates have regularly asked me to write articles, offer quotes, do interviews, and make presentations on the topics of networking, connecting, building a strong reputation, and attracting referrals. I also receive regular requests for consulting. These clients have similar questions: "How do I get more connected? How do I meet the right people? How do I hear about the good jobs? How can I get better referrals and clients?" This book answers many of those questions.

The Intentional Networker contains not only my experiences and thoughts on attracting and building quality business relationships, but also perspectives gleaned from savvy colleagues. It also includes real world stories, tips, and techniques that I've developed and practiced on the course of my journey. To date, that journey includes nearly three thousand business and networking events, including conferences, workshops, luncheons, coffees, happy hours, awards dinners, galas, fundraisers, and other gatherings.

In documenting, sorting through, and categorizing everything I know about how to network more intentionally, I came up with nine strategically ordered chapters. Each provides you with valuable, need-to-know information on how to network with greater purpose, focus, and polish. You may be surprised to discover that the first three chapters of this book aren't even about networking. They cover the important prerequisite work of self-discovery, setting intentions and goals, and building an authentic, credible brand that's in alignment with what you seek. These are necessary preparations before you head out the door to any networking event. After all, if others can't readily sense who you are, what you need, what you do better than anyone else, and what you're excited about, they probably won't "get" you, remember you, find you credible, or feel comfortable referring others to you.

While you may be tempted to skip these first few chapters, I encourage you to visit them anyway. The information they contain may be valuable if not critical to achieving the real results you want from your networking efforts. In fact, each chapter exists for a specific reason and is presented in an order that is both strategic and deliberate. The chapter on how to attract more referrals, which ultimately seems to be the topic everyone is most interested in, is the last chapter. The reason for this is that there are many lessons to learn and skills to build before it's appropriate to ask others to refer, trust, and bet their reputations on you.

You may note that I share many philosophies with other networking and business relationship experts. On the other hand, you'll also find some of my views to be different, even opposite. For example, I understand that one networking expert has the philosophy of never eating alone. While I respect that, my philosophy is hey, eat alone if you feel like eating alone. Every moment doesn't have to be a networking moment. You don't have to meet or get to know everyone in the room or go to lunch or coffee with everyone who asks. Sometimes we need a break from people and some time alone. I know I do. It's okay.

My ultimate wish is that you find *The Intentional Networker* to be helpful and filled with tips and strategies you can put to use immediately, easily, and regularly. Whether you read it cover to cover, or in bits and pieces, I hope it's the most valuable networking book you've ever read and helps you attract more powerful relationships, referrals, and results in business.

CHAPTER **I**

✳ know who you are

THE ESSENTIAL BASIS FOR SUCCESSFUL NETWORKING

In this chapter, you will:

- Get to know your authentic self and
  define your life's mission and purpose.

- Identify your standards, beliefs, and values.

- Discover why self-knowledge is essential
  to successful networking.

After being in business for more than ten years, Jason decided to expand his business. In the past, Jason had kept his company small and local. He focused on two specific services and had two part-time employees. The business was profitable and Jason had earned a sterling reputation in the local business community. He knew the expansion was a good move, but he also knew it would bring new challenges. So he hired a business consultant to provide objective guidance.

Jason was certain his consultant would start out by asking about his business plan and financials. He was surprised when the topic of his first session centered on self-discovery. Jason's consultant asked him to take two personality tests, review the results, and then schedule a weekend retreat away from the distractions of family, friends, and work. The consultant wanted Jason to focus and invest time getting clear on who he was as a person and what his talents and strengths were. The consultant also wanted Jason to do some assigned reading, complete several self-discovery exercises, create a list of core values and beliefs, develop a mission statement for his life and work, and develop a decade-by-decade vision for his life.

"At first I wasn't sure why this consultant asked me to do all this. I'd never done anything like it before," says Jason. "I soon learned that I had to get very clear on who I was, what made me tick, and what was important to me before I could be clear on any big decisions regarding my business." Jason also found that the exercises would help him spot and let go of anything dragging him down or creating roadblocks between him and success.

"Doing this work marked a dramatic turning point in my career and my life," says Jason "Everything changed after that. There was a definite shift in my attitude, my energy, and my outlook. I became more focused, purposeful, and discerning about everything."

Today Jason frequently goes back to what he documented about himself so he can refine and leverage it in his life and work. Those who know and do business with Jason have noted that his reputation and "stock" in the business community took off right about the time he began doing this work.

"Jason is full of positive energy and seems more focused now," says his friend Carol. "He's clear on his beliefs and standards. You know that he is all about integrity and purpose. People respect who he is, how he runs his business, and who and what he recommends to his clients and colleagues. They really trust him and his judgment."

Isn't this what you want others to say about you?

the value of self-knowledge

In working and connecting with others, both in personal and professional situations, you can spot the people who have – and have not – done the work that Jason did. This is the work of discovering and understanding who they are, why they're here, what they believe in, and what they want to accomplish in their lives.

The people who have invested in this self-examination work will have a vibrant energy about them. They work with purpose. They get things done. They're "on fire." Others find them attractive and enjoyable to know, talk to, and do business with. They are energizers who shine, sparkle, and project an aura of authentic joy.

People who know themselves are usually *not* the lost and negative people who complain about being unhappy or bored, the victims who rely on excuses or dwell on past wrongs, the emotional vampires who drain your energy, or the wallflowers who wait in the wings hoping something good will happen to them.

Another observation about people who know themselves: good

things tend to happen to them. It's not just luck. It's the culmination of focused energy, intention, a healthy measure of self-confidence and self-acceptance, a sense of purpose and integrity, and the phenomenon of positive attraction. Yes, these people have difficulties like anyone else, but when facing challenges, they handle them capably. Furthermore, they have strong support systems and they recover with resilience, learn the lessons, and look back on any adversity with a sense of grace.

In general, the people who know and understand themselves also have set high standards. They are happy, focused, and driven, and yet they also tend to be generous and care about others. Their lives are not just about them. They are part of something bigger than themselves. Furthermore, they remain open to continuing their journey of learning and self-discovery because they know the residual benefits this work brings.

What can you do to become more self-aware and enjoy the benefits of what some of the most successful people attract so readily? A good way is to follow these three basic steps:

※ **Discover who you are**

※ **Determine your mission or purpose**

※ **Clarify your beliefs and standards**

Whether you're on a tranquil retreat away from the busy-ness and distractions of work and life, flowing along in your daily routine, or in the midst of stress and upheaval, any time is an excellent time to discover, rediscover, or reassess your strengths, weaknesses, preferences, passions, fears, philosophies, standards, and policies.

But I warn you – it can be a complex and sometimes emotional task. As human beings we can be hard to define, our lives are fraught with "stuff," time and experiences have impacted us, and no two of us are exactly alike. You are a combination of nature, nurture, education, influence, and experience. And you are a moving target, always learning and evolving.

Self-discovery doesn't happen overnight. Nor is it ever a completed task that you can scratch off your To Do List.

But it's an exciting journey. So let's get started!

* * *

Self-discovery is a process and a journey,
not a once-and-done task.

* * *

discover who you are

Knowing yourself is about self-exploration: identifying, analyzing, celebrating, and leveraging your special gifts, strengths, and preferences. It's also about uncovering, acknowledging, understanding, accepting, and respecting your weaknesses, quirks, and fears. To know who you are is to understand why you do certain things in certain ways. It encompasses many dimensions, including your traits, talents, tendencies, preferences, passions, pet peeves, communication style, work style, emotional intelligence (how you react and respond to various situations), your energy flow, and even your "issues." Your unique DNA and your distinctive collection of life experiences combine into a recipe that makes you special and one-of-a-kind.

There are many ways to discover this wonderful being. Here are just a few of them.

Take personality profiles.

There are many different types of personality profiling tools available, and each is designed to show you different facets of yourself. I strongly suggest you take more than one. To date, I have taken the Myers-Briggs®, Birkman®, Enneagram, DISC®, and BarOn EQ-i® profiles. Each profile has taught me something new and valuable about myself, how I work, how I process information, how I interact with others, and much more.

Get capable support for the process of self-discovery.

Make no mistake: taking a good look at you can be exciting, but it can also be emotional. So when taking any tests and doing this important exploratory work, consider working under the guidance of a certified professional. You can also participate in facilitated retreats. These can give you the dedicated space and time to work through a variety of self-discovery exercises with the help of facilitators and fellow attendees.

Inventory your strengths and talents.

We all have natural gifts. Sometimes these gifts are obvious; sometimes they are more subtle. Maybe you are creative, funny, a good listener, or a whiz at numbers. Think about areas where certain activities or situations are easy and energizing for you, even if you assume that everyone can do them with ease. (Trust me, they probably can't!)

Enlist the help of others in your strength and talent inventory. One of my favorite sayings is, "You can't read the label if you're stuck inside the jar." We just can't see ourselves in an objective and accurate way. That's why it's so important to ask trusted friends, family, and colleagues to reflect back to you (as truthfully and objectively as they can) what they see as your special strengths, talents, and gifts. You may be pleasantly surprised at the feedback they share with you.

> Asking for honest, objective feedback from others is a great way to see yourself and your traits, gifts, and strengths. It gives you a valuable new perspective.

Face and assess your weaknesses, fears, and areas for growth.

It's easy to avoid that which scares you or makes you feel uncomfortable or inadequate. It's also much less stressful (in the short run anyway) to avoid, ignore, deny, or otherwise hide from your weaknesses and faults. But come on. Wouldn't it be smarter and nobler to face and accept them, forgive them, pat them on the head, learn from them, shore them up as best you can, and move on?

Assess your own feelings, behavior, energizers, and drainers.

Take notes regarding your energy level and mood under certain situations and with certain people. When do you feel the happiest and most energized? What sucks the life out of you? What repels you? What makes your gut or heart hurt? What makes you angry? What reactions do you have to certain situations and people? This information is necessary and valuable to your quest for self-knowledge and understanding.

Review and inventory your background and experience.

Assess your professional experience and talents as well as your personal and educational background. List every little thing you've done and learned along the way. What did you enjoy? What did you ace? What drove you nuts or was a struggle? Note the disparities and patterns.

try this!

Revisit who you were as a child. Opinions vary on which age to revisit, your five-year-old, eight-year-old, or even thirteen-year-old self. I say pick the age at which you recall being the happiest. What were you like at that age? What did you enjoy? What was your favorite way to play? How did you see yourself? What were your interests and joys? Your struggles and fears? Take notes on what you discover here. You may be startled to find how far you've drifted from your inner child. Or what strong feelings still resonate.

determine your mission or purpose

Finding your mission, also called your life purpose, is about learning why you're here and how you can put your special combination of gifts, talents, experiences, and passions to work to make a positive impact on the world.

A dear friend, Sue Cullen, called this "Mattering." She believed that who you are and what you do every day really does *matter* to others and to the world. As a career consultant and executive coach, her joy was helping others discover and develop their special gifts and find greater purpose and higher meaning in their lives and work. This could mean embarking on a huge project impacting thousands of people or simply making a conscious, consistent choice to be kind and respectful to others every day. Sue passed away in 2010 but her legacy of "Mattering" lives on.

As Sue saw firsthand, when you discover your mission, an amazing thing happens: you become exponentially energized and focused. Getting up each morning is exciting and purposeful. Work doesn't feel so much like work. It's easier to get through times of doubt and difficulty. It's an authentic paradigm shift.

* * *

*Purpose brings new passion to our lives and
helps guide and focus our choices and actions. It is the
foundation for being more intentional in all we do.*

* * *

Defining your mission is *not* a waste of time. If anyone tries to tell you that it's a frivolous, pointless, or selfish pursuit, ignore them. Discovering and developing your mission statement is part of living your best life and making the most of your brief visit to Planet Earth.

> Here is my mission statement at this writing. It has evolved substantially over the last decade and continues to evolve, but that's okay. It guides, energizes, and helps me focus on what's important each day. "My mission is to use my gifts, experiences, and resources to empower others to become more purposeful, successful, and fulfilled as they make a positive impact on the world."

Develop your own mission statement.

There are many good books and resources available to help you with this task, which won't happen overnight and may require updates from time to time. The book that got me started was Laurie Beth Jones' best seller, *The Path: Creating Your Mission Statement for Work and Life*. The book is written from a Christian perspective, but its messages and exercises have the power to resonate with people of any belief system. If this book doesn't work for you, there are certainly others. The important thing is to get started.

If you want to create a personal mission statement as well as one for your business or job, please note: even if they are separate, they should align in some way. The belief that it's possible to be one person at work and another in your non-working hours is a myth. It's definitely possible that work allows you to bring forth a certain part of yourself that you don't get to share in your personal life and vice versa. But your basic beliefs should still be aligned whether you are on the job or at home. Otherwise there will be dissonance – not only unhealthy, but confusing.

Make a list of activities you love to do.

What do you enjoy so much that you lose all track of time and become completely absorbed? What leaves you feeling energized? Create a list of these activities. They can be tasks you do at home or at work, things you do as a hobby or as a volunteer, or things you do to relax with family and friends. This list will provide clues as to what your mission is and what suits you.

Richard Nelson Bolles notes in his book, *What Color is Your Parachute: A Practical Manual for Job Hunters and Career Changers,* that your mission, even if you believe it is pre-ordained, should be something that appeals to you. Something you delight in. Free will is part of the process. So don't limit yourself to thoughts of what you think you should do. A valid mission statement includes what you love to do.

Describe your perfect day in your perfect job.

What are you doing? Who are you working with and serving? What are you accomplishing? How is it changing lives or the world? How does it make you feel? What are you experiencing?

> The description of your perfect work day will reveal clues as to what your mission is. What are you doing? Who are you serving? What results are you creating?

try this!

Write your own headstone inscription, obituary, and eulogy. Sounds morbid, but this can be a life changer. If you were allowed only eight to ten words to carve on your headstone, what would you like those words to be? Now live the life that matches this. Similarly, write your own obituary, not just as it would be today, but as you hope it will be. What's missing? What clues does this give you to your life purpose? Finally, at your funeral, what do you want your friends, family, and colleagues to say about you? What will they remember most about you? In what ways will you have impacted others? What were your contributions to the world? This is the legacy you leave behind – your place in history. What do you want it to be?

clarify your beliefs, values, and standards

Once you have a reasonable grasp on who you are and what your mission and purpose is, move to the next step: contemplating, clarifying, and recording your beliefs and standards. Some call these your core values.

These beliefs, values, and standards are the things you feel most passionate about. They are your must-haves and deal breakers. They are the things that make you feel good when you do them or see them; they are the things that upset or infuriate you when you don't. They are the standards that you will uphold in your life and work, for yourself and for others; the things you believe in, stand up for, and do. No matter what.

Here are some simple (notice I didn't say easy) ways to examine your beliefs, standards, and values.

Start a collection of quotes, sayings, or passages that resonate with you.

I began collecting quotes and phrases back in high school. I logged these little gems in a notebook, which I still have, and am still adding to. The quotes come from many sources: family sayings, greeting cards, presentations, ancient literature, homilies, books, magazines, television shows, movies, songs, ads, bumper stickers, t-shirts, and even wise and witty friends. I add anything that speaks to my heart, makes me think, makes me laugh, inspires me, comforts me, or makes me say, "Wow! I love that!"

Make a list of people you admire.

This list can include friends, family, teachers, mentors, colleagues, clients, leaders in your community, people with whom you do business, historic figures, musicians, authors, celebrities, sports figures, and so on.

Why do you feel drawn to these people? Learn from them, let them inspire you, and understand that they are a reflection of your best self! Note what you admire and appreciate about each person on your list.

* * *

Look all around you. You will find some of the most inspiring role models in the most ordinary and humble places.

* * *

Create a list of companies and organizations you admire.

You're probably hearing a lot about branding in the business world – having a memorable brand, building your brand, leveraging your brand, rebranding, and so on. But what does it mean? My short answer is that the businesses and organizations you deal with will leave an impression on you. What is that impression? Make a list of the businesses where you have a consistently positive experience, whether it's a restaurant, retail store, or service. Note what it is you like about them and why you keep going back.

why do this work?

When you invest time in this self-discovery work you begin a wonderful and ongoing journey.

> Self-knowledge makes it easier to find your authentic self, set more appropriate goals and intentions, live and work in integrity, target opportunities for further learning and growth, and stimulate the power of synchronicity.

Self-knowledge also improves your ability to deal with problems and challenges with greater resilience and grace. It's a lifelong journey that confers innumerable benefits, not the least of which is to attract people who will enhance or illuminate your life and business. That's what networking is for, right?

You will become clear on what makes you unique and special.

Self-discovery helps you make friends with your core essence and spirit. You become more aware of your own special and authentic blend of strengths, weaknesses, beliefs, and preferences. You can then stop comparing yourself to others or beating yourself up as you try to be (or become) someone you aren't. You begin to accept and embrace *you*. After all, you are unlike anyone else who has ever walked this planet, then, now, or in years to come. When you are clear, others can be clear about you too.

> When you take the time to examine, acknowledge, leverage,
> and celebrate who you truly are, it can lead you on an
> amazing journey. You discover the special ways you and
> you alone were destined to impact others and the world.

You will gain clarity in your passions and beliefs.

Taking time for self-discovery allows you to explore and pinpoint what's most important to you, what brings you joy and energy, and what you will and will not suffer. Finding this clarity grants you the power and focus to build a life, find engaging and purposeful work, and attract and build honest relationships that are collaborative, productive, and meaningful. This leads to a greater sense of urgency, focus, and passion for you and respect and appreciation from others.

You'll live with more authenticity and integrity.

You can't be authentic, genuine, and sincere if you don't know, understand, and honor your true self, and feel clear and confident in your beliefs. Doing this in an age of showiness and false pretense is rare, refreshing, and healthy.

You'll discover and honor what's best for you. Trying to live or work as others want you to can be exhausting, depressing, and terribly ineffective. Certainly you can learn from and be inspired by others. But ideally the goal is to develop your *own* unique approach to living and working; one that feels right and natural to you and brings you joy, energy, and fulfillment.

You will find the power of walking your talk. Ever deal with someone who was the poster child for "Do as I say, not as I do?" Dealing with someone who does not walk their talk is not only confusing, but draining, frustrating, and off-putting. Demonstrating what you believe in with your words *and* actions is what earns respect from others. It's one of the many traits you'll find in admired, respected, and effective leaders.

You become more energized and exude healthy confidence.

When you can see, appreciate, and celebrate yourself and then understand how you are meant to create an impact on the world, it's not only energizing, it gives you a sense of purpose, value, and confidence. Who else can do what you do and in exactly the same way that you do it? Who else has had your unique experiences? No one! That's what makes each of us so special and valuable. Isn't that worth celebrating?

You will experience less dissonance and stress.

Ever been asked to do or be something that just didn't feel right? It probably made you feel uncomfortable or filled with pain or guilt. Maybe it drained your energy or even made you physically sick. This dissonance is unhealthy on many levels.

Michelle experienced this in her early career as an opera singer. She entered the world of professional opera at just seventeen, which was a dream come true – at first. Then as Michelle matured, got to know herself better, and faced some uncomfortable situations, she saw that a career on the stage was not for her. She did some exploring, changed course, and found a new and engaging career. Her experiences in the world of opera divas, combined with several other work experiences, led her to a fascination with how humans and organizations operate. She went back to school to study organizational development. Today Michelle runs a thriving consulting practice where she empowers individuals and organizations to develop their vision, core values, and mission statements.

"Were it not for my previous experiences and understanding what I wanted and what I didn't, I don't think I would be standing where I am today," Michelle says. "Being true to yourself, your interests, and your standards is the only way to live and work. It helps you recognize when opportunities, situations, or relationships are or are not right for you and what you can do about it."

If you don't have this level of self-knowledge you will mostly likely feel like you are struggling. Or you will mistake being busy or stressed for being productive. Or worse, you will live and do business in ways that are boring, unappealing, uncomfortable, exhausting, disappointing, ineffective, superficial, and in some cases questionable. Could this be you? If so, it's time for a change!

You'll enjoy a firmer foundation for better decisions.

Have you ever struggled with a decision, impulsively said yes or no to a request, or launched into a major project, commitment, or relationship without being clear on the mission and what it meant to you?

Self-discovery helps you make better decisions in everything you do. It helps you say yes or no at the right time. Furthermore, it helps you say it clearly and confidently. Others can see you mean it. Discussion closed. Manipulation and guilt averted. What a relief!

This decision-making ranges from the miniscule (whether to eat that cheesecake placed in front of you at a business luncheon) to the life-altering (whether to launch that company, accept that job, or marry that potential mate). It helps you assess whether you're aligned with your purpose – or not. It helps you know who you can help and how.

Knowing yourself and your mission and clarifying what's important to you can help you decide who "your people" are, what books you read, how you spend your time, and even how you present yourself. It can help you make decisions about associations, actions, choices, jobs, clients, products and services. It can even help you choose your words.

You can set and keep priorities with more consistency. Sooner or later you will realize you're not given an endless amount of time, energy, or resources. You just can't do it all. That's when knowing who you are and understanding the best use of your energy, time, and talents can help you set priorities and select what you want and need to do first. Everything else will have to wait – or be handled by someone else.

You stay more focused and on track. Call it your road map, your North Star, or even your onboard GPS; your self-knowledge helps you set your sights and move ahead, steadily and on track. It guides you along the journey, keeping you headed in the right direction. It helps you know what you are attracted to and why. It shows you how to spot something you can or cannot (or should not) do, endorse, or support – and why. There is both relief and satisfaction in finally becoming clear and knowing where you're going. You can respect and manage your life and work with greater clarity and ease. You can relax just a bit and let it guide you. You know it will always be there to light the way.

You can more easily identify and attract like-minded people.

With your standards in place, you can make better choices about whether or not you want to connect with, associate with, work with, or recommend certain people or companies. It helps you know who or what to avoid and who you want to attract. If you are aware of what grabs your attention and attracts you, be it a genuine smile, a warm and generous heart, or shared interests, you can begin the process of refining your connections, relationships, and referrals.

* * *

Knowing yourself helps you assess yourself, and it is also helpful in observing and assessing others.

* * *

When you are clear on who you are, what your purpose is, and what you believe, you will find that you attract and achieve greater success, meaning, and drive because you are working from something that resonates deep within you. You are more passionate, focused, and determined. You will find that you have greater energy behind your actions and relationships. You will not only be more fulfilled, but also much more attractive to others.

Self-knowledge is important to the premise of working, connecting, and referring at a higher level. Without it, successful networking is not possible. It is the basis and beginning of truly becoming an Intentional Networker.

CHAPTER **2**

✳ set your vision, intentions, and goals

WHAT DO YOU *REALLY* WANT?

In this chapter, you will:

- Learn how to get clearer on what you want.

- Understand the power of being purposeful and why this is an absolute must for successful networking.

- Set goals and intentions that align with who you are.

When Jane was in college back in the 1970s, she was an avid article-clipper and creator of collages. She cut out photos, drawings, and even words that she thought were inspiring and indicative of what she wanted in her life. This was long before the concept of vision boards became as popular and mainstream as it is today.

As she neared her college graduation date, Jane cut out a photo from a magazine that captured the essence of what she wanted next. It showed a woman sitting at a desk with colorful art and photos tacked on the bulletin board behind her. She was well-dressed and wore stylish glasses. Her feet were clad in designer heels and propped up on a beautiful wood desk. She was smiling – almost laughing – while talking on the phone, looking confident, capable, and happy. Jane glued the photo to a card and tucked it away in a file marked "Career."

Fifteen years later, Jane was going through her files as she prepared to move to a new home. She found the file and the photo of the woman with her feet propped up on the desk. She had not looked at it in fifteen years. "My jaw just dropped," Jane said. "I realized that this woman was me. The hair, the glasses, the clothes, the office, even the shoes. I'd already been that "me" as an executive at an advertising agency. I just couldn't believe how powerful that vision was, despite it being tucked away all these years, and how I'd absolutely nailed it. Since I had just left that advertising job, I knew it was time to envision what was next in my life and to revisit the powerful practice of visualizing and recording what I wanted."

the importance of knowing what you want

It's so hard to watch: people you care about wandering through life without any idea of what they really want or need or how they will get there, let alone how they want to use their talents to positively impact the world. I am frequently approached by people who want to tap into my expertise and connections to locate their next big opportunity, but often these people have no solid idea of what they are seeking. They have no clear vision, no intentions or goals mapped out. It's hard to help them when they show this kind of ambivalence.

If you have no purpose, direction, vision, or goals, then you might end up on a treadmill going nowhere. You'll lurch along, taking on work that is boring or unsatisfying. You may find yourself taking on burdens and roles you never wanted. Could this be you? I really hope not! But there are lots of people like this roaming the planet.

In the movie *Thelma & Louise*, Louise tells Thelma, "You get what you settle for." She tells Thelma to quit limping along aimlessly, without standards or goals, living from day to day, minute to minute, making random and often ill-fated decisions, and letting others, including her emotional midget of a husband, run (and ruin) her life. It's time for Thelma to get herself together, devote some time to figuring out what *she* wants in life, grow a spine, and go after her dreams!

* * *

It's true: you do get what you settle for.

* * *

Here's the truth: you can't achieve, attract, or receive any assistance from God, the Universe, colleagues, mentors, friends, family, or even professionals you hire, if you don't have a clue what you want. The way to change this is to create your vision, understand and name your intentions, and set some goals.

vision

So what is vision? It's the long-range picture of what you want in your life. It can be a literal image such as a sketch, photo, collage, or vision board. It can be something you've written down in words. Or it simply can be an image you have in your mind's eye. Having a vision means you have a dream or a picture of what you want to see for yourself in the future. You're the arrow, and your vision is the target.

In the sports world, particularly in games like soccer or football, you may hear about athletes who have good "field vision." This means they can see the big picture of what's going on across the entire field. They see what each player is doing and can anticipate the next moves of the game. This person is not in just one place or in one moment of the game, but in many places at once, thinking ahead. The most successful athletes in team sports have this vision.

What kind of vision do you have? Are you living from moment to moment? Day to day? Job to job? Paycheck to paycheck? Relationship to relationship? If so, your vision is severely nearsighted. Or perhaps you enjoy dreaming about the future and what you wish for, yet can't see the steps you must take to achieve those dreams. In that case, your vision is far-sighted. Maybe you have a vague idea of what your future could be like, but it's all hazy and unfocused. In this case, your vision could be like someone who suffers from astigmatism or glaucoma.

Having vision in the literal sense has to do with our eyes, but it's also about using our minds, hearts, and imaginations. Having a vision means you think about, long for, sense, or "see" something up ahead. It's what leads you and drives you each day as you make decisions and plans and take action.

My friend Tara spoke of vision one night when she was hosting a gathering of mutual friends. Everything about the gathering was lovely; the colors and décor in her new home, the delicious and well-presented food and beverages. Nothing was over-the-top or excessively fancy. It was just appealing, beautiful, delicious, and done in a seemingly effortless way. The conversation and laughter flowed.

I asked Tara for her secret. How did she create such a special evening? She replied, "Well, I think you have to start with a vision." That was more than ten years ago and I still hear Tara's words when I am trying to create something new or update something old, whether it's planning a good meal, redecorating a room, designing a new promotional piece for my business, or mapping out a client's project. You must start with a vision. After that, the next steps fall more easily into place.

try this!

Create a vision board or collage. If you're a visual person, you will love this activity. There are professional coaches and consultants who offer facilitated workshops on how to create a vision board, but you can do it yourself at home. Simply collect words and images that spark something in you, capturing the essence of what you want in your life or your work. Then paste these words and images onto poster board or cardboard in whatever way you want. This is a productive way to utilize magazines before they go into the recycling bin, and it's a fun, insightful, and purposeful way to spend time with friends and colleagues. All you need is magazines, scissors, glue, and some heavy paper or cardboard. Break out the coffee, tea, or even cocktails and have fun with it.

Some experts believe you should put your completed collage/vision board where you can see it and be inspired by it. Others say the power of the vision board is in its creation and it's not necessary to view it each day. Jane's story shows that just choosing the images and words is powerful by itself.

intentions

You can find many definitions for the word "intention." Here's one from The American Heritage Dictionary, Third Edition: "intention is a course of action that one intends to follow ... an aim that guides an action."

Intentions are mindsets. They are what you ask for, what you purport to be, what you are determined to do, and where you intend to go. They are your long-range plans based on the vision you've imagined or created. They may be your prayers and wishes for yourself or others.

In her book *Secrets of Six-Figure Women*, Barbara Stanny describes intentions as declarations. They are decisions, statements, resolutions, pronouncements, even manifestos. You are deciding how things are going to be. You are opening to the possibility that whatever you're doing, it can be bold and big. And it's with the attitude that your intentions *will* happen. You can choose it!

Dianna Amorde, author of *Aha! Moments: When Intellect and Intuition Collide*, has a lot to say about intentions and how powerful they are. "The best intentions are those inspired from the wisdom of your heart and intuitive right brain and tend to be rather general," Dianna says. "These intentions allow your intuition to speak and invite God or the Universe to handle the details in ways you can't begin to imagine or explain."

Intentions allow for some flexibility, serendipity, and synchronicity as to how they might be achieved. They acknowledge that your human, singular vision may be myopic. Setting an intention helps you see what may not be readily obvious to you.

try this!

My colleague Leia Francisco, a coach, consultant, and author of *Writing Through Transitions*, shared this simple but profound exercise with me. Make a list of one hundred things you want to do or have in your life, business, or career. Yes, one hundred. Even if they may seem unfeasible right now. Check the list every thirty days or every quarter. Note what you've achieved or what's shown up for you via synchronicity.

goals

Goals are different from vision and intentions, but are sometimes confused with them. Vision involves creating the broad strokes, thinking long-range, and understanding the big picture. Intentions are statements about your visions that are distinct, but allow for some flexibility and freedom as to how they will be achieved, who will be involved, and even how they might be expanded upon.

In contrast, goals involve specific, tangible, detailed, measurable, and action-oriented steps. They have details attached to them, as well as benchmarks and deadlines. Goals tend to be more logical and concrete. They involve planning, organizing, and actual *doing*.

Goal-setting involves determining the parameters of the goal and deciding what steps you must take to accomplish them. This can involve many steps and require that you develop certain habits and consistently make certain choices. Commitment to the goal is critical.

Having intentions without the necessary goals to achieve them is like deciding to take a trip and even choosing the destination, but then never doing the research, setting a date, making the reservations, booking the flights, gassing up the car, packing your bags, or actually setting forth on the journey.

* * *

Goals give intentions form, details, action, and a timetable.

* * *

On the other hand, goals without intentions are just achievements without any specific passion or purpose behind them. You're just busy, but you don't know why. And you never quite feel like you're making any progress. Goals without purpose or intent are tiring, joyless, and dreary. You're busy, but not going anywhere you want to go.

Create lists of goals and next steps, even baby steps, for your intentions and wishes – and act on them.

There are many stories in books or movies that may give you the impression that all you have to do is dream something up and it will happen. Not so. Although it says in the Bible, "Ask and you shall receive," this is just the first step - the second is action. Actions show commitment. What specifically are you going to do to ensure that you achieve your vision and intentions? What commitment is required on your part? What actions will you take? Write them down. And then do them.

how vision, intentions, and goals work together

Let's say you spot a recipe in a magazine. You are drawn to the photo of the finished dish, including the mouth-watering food, the elegant serving dishes, exciting garnish, and colorful table centerpiece. This is the vision. It evokes an emotional response in you.

Your vision becomes an intention when you decide to create this dish and serve it to your family or friends. You may even announce that this is your intention, creating desire for this scrumptious dish in others as well. You're not sure how you're going to pull it off or when, but you know you will.

When it's time to set your goals and make your vision a reality, the goals will include details such as purchasing the necessary ingredients, following the recipe instructions, and serving the dish to your friends in your home, on the date and time you have set on your calendar.

But wait! Before you even get to these details, your best friend, who happens to be in training as a chef, has just heard you speak of your vision and intent regarding this recipe. She saw it in the same publication. What a coincidence! She needs to practice for an upcoming practical cooking test and offers to come over, help you create this meal, and give you pointers on how you can do it yourself next time.

There's more – a few days before your dinner event, you pass by a store on the way to a dentist appointment. They have the very dishes used in the magazine photo on display. And they're on sale! You step inside and buy them. Suddenly it's like everyone and everything is conspiring to help you achieve your vision. In a way they are. But you're also "tuned in" to what you want so you spot the right signals and opportunities, act on them (this is important), and achieve your vision a little more easily. That's the power of vision at work along with the power of setting distinct intentions and measurable goals.

How do vision, intentions, and goals apply specifically to business? Here are some sample sentences that show this:

Vision: "I can see myself doing the work I love, working from an office in my home, having the freedom to be my own boss, being there for my kids, making the kind of money I want and deserve to make, working with clients and colleagues I enjoy, and making a difference in people's lives."

Intention: "I intend to find a way to do the work I love, have an office at home, have the freedom to be my own boss, be there for my kids, make the kind of money I want to make, work with clients and colleagues I enjoy, and make a difference in people's lives."

Goal: "I will open my own communications business within the next year, turn our guest room into my office, be my own boss, work thirty hours a week, be there when my kids get home from school, make $75,000 per year, and work with clients and colleagues who are smart, savvy, and creative and who I have met via focused networking and marketing activities."

try this!

Develop a manifesto, a list of dreams and declarations, or even start a dedicated journal, about your vision, intentions, and goals. Make it fun, positive, liberating, even outrageous.

clarity

Like a good pair of eyeglasses, clarity of mind can change everything about how you "see." My colleague Ann Daly, Ph.D., is a former professor at The University of Texas at Austin and now an executive coach, keynote speaker, and author. Dr. Daly focuses much of her work around this topic and says being really clear on who you are and what you want is where you gain your true strength and power.

"Having clarity is about being grounded; knowing the plot of ground you stand on," Dr. Daly says. "And the more grounded you are the less you worry about pleasing other people. Furthermore when you're grounded you can't be pulled off balance as easily."

How do you achieve clarity? One way is to set aside the quiet, introspective time that allows you to figure out what it is.

Set aside time for stillness.

Life is full of opportunities to be busy and distracted. It's easy to create To Do lists and calendars that are jammed with tasks and appointments that may have absolutely nothing to do with your mission, vision, intentions, or goals. No wonder it's so easy to begin the day feeling overwhelmed, and then end the day believing you've done nothing worthwhile.

try this!

Schedule and invest in regular meditative time, whether it's scheduling a quarterly weekend retreat or setting aside fifteen minutes every day. It's hard to be inspired, creative, clear, and at ease if your mind is constantly cluttered. Think of this as clearing out the junk drawer of your mind. During this special time you can pray, walk in the woods, listen to soothing music, do yoga, or meditate on your vision, intentions, and goals. Let your mind be free, if only for a few minutes. Take note of what happens.

priorities

When I turned forty, "prioritize" became one of my favorite words. As a busy, entrepreneurial mom, I realized I only had so much time and energy each day. I just could not have it all or do it all, at least not all at once. Furthermore, I couldn't please everyone or solve everyone else's problems. I had to get real with myself and figure out what I could achieve and what was important to me.

Thank goodness, I took the time to figure out what my vision, intentions, goals, and *priorities* really were. This strategizing simply was not optional for me – and what a revelation it was.

Right about that time I received some monumental advice from Hope J. Lafferty, author of *Organizing Workspace A to Z*. She revealed to me one of her secrets:

> Most human beings can realistically only focus on three key areas of their life at any given time. Just three. That is, if they want to remain healthy, happy, and sane.

My Big Three priorities were: 1) personal wellness and self care, 2) home and family, and 3) my business and life's work. Once I nailed these down, I started keeping a running list of the three top intentions and goals for each item. After that, it became so much easier for me to say yes to what was important to me and a firm, no-guilt, no-regrets no to anything that was not. It took time, and I still have to work on this each day, but it has given me clarity.

Yes, I still spend quality time with friends and colleagues, have some hobbies I enjoy, and serve my community regularly, but there are a lot of things that don't make my Priority List anymore. What are *your* Big Three?

try this!

Use a target to help you set your priorities. Draw a target (a circle with concentric circles within). Leave a circle large enough to write in at the center. Starting at the center, write the #1 most important thing in your life – the thing that you absolutely must have if all else goes to hell. In the next circle from the center, write the one or two things that mean the most to you and that you must have in your life to get through the day. Go out another circle and write two or three things that are next on your importance list. Continue in this manner, adding more to each circle as you move toward the outside of the target.

You'll find that the center and the inner two or three circles are the items you are most likely to focus on. The items on the outside may get your attention and energy, but only when the inner items are fulfilled. (Hint: you may want to use a pencil for this as you might be erasing and rewriting.)

the to do list

You've got a vision, have set your intentions, and stated some concrete goals and priorities. Now what? The next step is to create your strategic To Do List, which includes your goals and deadlines and the various steps and tasks that go along with them.

Maybe you have some To Do items on your current list that don't align perfectly with your vision and intentions. This is worth reviewing and thinking about. Do all those action items *really* need to be there? If so, ask yourself "why?" It's a liberating feeling to cross something off your list because you realize it simply doesn't have to be done.

: Be sure the items on your To Do List help you take action and
: make progress every day toward your vision and intentions,
: or you'll be pulled off the path pretty quickly.

When you make good decisions on a regular and routine basis (and by "good" I mean decisions that move you incrementally toward your vision, intentions, and goals), these eventually become good habits. Your To Do list may contain items that seem small and insignificant, but they add up quickly to deliver significant progress toward meeting your goals and manifesting your intentions.

try this!

Consider creating an intentional, if not feisty, Don't Do List. This serves as a reminder to stop doing things that don't matter to you and possibly aren't even yours to deal with. What are the ways you waste time and energy? Write these down, and then don't do them.

why do this work?

Know where you are going.

With your mission, vision, intentions, and goals in place, you will have a purposeful game plan that helps you efficiently and mindfully channel your time, resources, and energies toward what matters to you. When you get clear on what you want, you are finally free to focus on it. You can be confident as you intentionally live your life, follow your dreams, build your career or run your business, make connections, build relationships, and make a lasting and positive impact on the world. You are in alignment with *your* unique mission, purpose, vision, intentions, and goals. People who have this clarity of purpose are attractive, inspiring, and energizing to others.

Become more efficient and productive.

Being busy for the sake of looking busy will be a thing of the past. When you make better choices you not only conserve and use your time and energy more wisely, you do the same with your money and other resources as well. You can also let go of needless clutter and deflect useless "noise." You will achieve more goals in less time and enjoy a higher success rate.

Attract and develop like-minded friends, colleagues, clients, and connections.

When you get really clear on what you want and what you're about, you may find a corresponding shift in what you want out of your relationships. You become more attracted to, and *attractive* to, those who are aligned with you or who complement you in positive ways.

Ultimately, it takes focus, drive, and discipline to do any of the work described in this chapter. It takes discipline to create your vision, intentions, and goals. It takes discipline to stop procrastinating, get focused, take action, and stay on course. But when you are clear and determined and know what you want, you will find a way to do it.

Start small and rejoice in each goal achieved. You will probably discover that if you are working toward something that is important to you, in alignment with who you are, and serves the world in a meaningful way, you will find the passion and energy needed to do the work. What's more, the work won't feel like work at all. What a surprise it will be to discover that it's actually fun and energizing – and helps you connect with others who can and want to help you!

❋ build an authentic, polished image and brand

ALIGN WHO YOU ARE WITH WHAT THEY SEE

In this chapter, you will:

- Learn how to build a brand that aligns with your vision, intentions, and goals.

- Know why it's critical to generate positive first impressions.

- Discover ways to strengthen your ability to attract high-quality relationships, customers, and colleagues.

Alice is a talented freelance writer with a delightful personality, a solid work ethic, and a keen attention to detail. When I first met her, most of her clients were local publishers and small businesses. She charged a modest hourly rate (or accepted whatever fee publications offered her), but loved the work and the freelance life. Her references were excellent, reflecting the quality of her work. Alice tended to be casual in her appearance, but that didn't seem to hamper her ability to attract the types of projects she initially wanted.

After having her first child and experiencing the usual challenges of being a new mom, Alice's attitude about work changed dramatically. She realized that to help support her child she needed to earn and contribute more money to the household. She and her husband had chosen to split childcare duties, so she wanted to make more money working fewer hours.

Alice came to me to help her develop some strategies on how she could adjust to the changes in her life and attract higher-paying corporate clients.

I was surprised when Alice came to our first meeting looking so casual. Her hair was dirty and carelessly twisted up in a clip. She wore no makeup, giving her a pale and tired appearance. Her shirt was worn, rumpled, and appeared to be her husband's. She wore a pair of faded jeans and flip-flop sandals, and carried a shapeless canvas purse that had seen better days. In short, Alice looked anything but professional and certainly not ready to present herself to or work for the corporate clients I had in mind for her. Yet Alice talked eagerly about her goals to add to her client list and make more money.

Having gone through the same new-mom adjustment myself years earlier, I could relate. Having a baby changes everything and finding the right balance between work and parenting is tricky. Yet I knew Alice had to wake up and regain control of her life, her image, and her career.

The first advice I gave Alice was to consider getting some loving and reliable childcare so she could have more time to focus on and be available to the clients she wanted to attract. The second tip I offered was to go shopping and purchase at least one, preferably two, polished outfits, a few coordinating separates and accessories to mix and match with the outfits, some dress shoes, and a professional purse or briefcase. I also recommended she get a flattering, up-to-date hairstyle and begin wearing a touch of makeup.

The goal was to give Alice a more polished, professional, capable, and current look, and to help her feel both comfortable and confident meeting with corporate clients. These were the clients who could afford to pay her the premium rates her peers made and give her the steady work she told me she wanted. In short, the changes I suggested would help her develop the professional image that aligned with her talents and goals.

Immediately Alice was resistant. She countered that she couldn't afford any of it. I assured her that while the items would definitely come with price tags, she might consider viewing the purchases as investments in her professional and financial future. It was about taking care of herself as well as her family in the manner she deserved and desired.

Still Alice balked. At that point, there was nothing more I could say or do but wish her well.

I ran into Alice again several months later. She had not made any of the changes I had suggested – not one – and still had the appearance of a struggling, worn-out mom. To make ends meet, she had taken a part-time job at a coffee shop that paid minimum wage and tips.

A year later, I heard from Alice again. She had applied for a part-time writing job that had the pay and hours that she believed were ideal for her situation. She *really* wanted this job. She had been invited in for an interview and was seeking my advice once again. I gave Alice the same advice: polish up, invest in some professional attire, and look the part. This time she listened. And guess what? She got the job. I wasn't surprised. Alice is a capable professional and talented communicator. She has so much to offer her clients. She just needed the professional image on the outside that matched the intelligence, experience, and professional vision she carried on the inside.

how you show up matters

Like Alice, people communicate many things about themselves which are not in line with what they say they want to project or are trying to attract.

You've probably experienced something like this situation. You meet someone at a networking event. You note that they are profession- ally dressed, well-groomed and "put together." You shake hands and look into the person's eyes. There's a sparkle there you like. You begin to converse and gain a sense of their personality; you learn what she does for a living and why she is at this particular event. There may be an immediate "click." The person is vibrant and engaging and exudes energy, confidence, and credibility. You enjoy the exchange. This person is "attractive" on several levels. She seems genuine and what she says verbally is congruent with the message you pick up non-verbally. You decide fairly quickly that you'd like to have her card and add her to your database, perhaps meet again and consider how you could do business together.

Or maybe you have another kind of experience in meeting some- one. This person may have shown up looking overly casual, poorly groomed, or otherwise ill-prepared for a professional setting. You might experience his handshake as limp, nervous, or overzealous. His words may not sound authentic or sincere. You may pick up on discomfort, insecurity, or uncertainty. Something's misaligned between what he says and how he appears. You are soon ready to move on to another conversation with someone else. Bottom line: something's not clicking. You experience confusion or dissonance instead of engagement or attraction.

> It's true. We do judge and evaluate others – and they do the same with us – based on first impressions, appearance, and initial interactions. It's what we humans are hardwired to do. We've been doing this for thousands of years. It used to be about survival of the species. Now it's about business.

You can be as skeptical as you like or comment on how shallow it may seem, but scientific and human behavior studies prove it over and over again: how you present yourself to the world does affect how others perceive you, react to you, and form opinions about you. Not only in first-impression situations, but also as relationships develop over time.

Whether it's via in-person interaction, conversations by telephone, written correspondence, posts and comments on social networking channels, or other communications, your personal image – your brand – sends signals and affects whether you will be successful in achieving what you want in your life and business.

Leadership communications expert and author David Grossman notes that everything we say and do – and everything we *don't* say and *don't* do – says something. Hence the title for his book, *You Can't Not Communicate.* He adds that the higher up we go, the more success we want to attract, the more we are watched and observed. The stakes get higher.

: What are you saying and doing, or not saying and not doing,
: that may be affecting your ability to attract and achieve what
: you want?

does your image and brand match who you are and what you want?

Your "personal brand" has been described as the unique blend of qualities and characteristics that make you distinctive and memorable; the traits that make you stand out from others around you. It's impacted by many facets and factors of how you look, act, communicate, conduct yourself, and run your business.

To serve you accurately and effectively, your brand must align with who you are, what you believe in, and what you're trying to achieve or attract. If it doesn't, it's amazing how quickly others will pick up on this "disconnect" and likely disregard you or not trust you. Therefore, it's important to always work at presenting your best, most authentic, and credible self.

first impressions: where it all begins

The first reactions people have to you, whether conscious or subconscious, in person or electronically, can impact how they feel about you for years to come. The time-honored saying, "You only get one chance to make a good first impression" is truer than ever. With that in mind, pay close attention to first-impression factors as you work to strengthen your brand and image.

materials and media

Given that we live in the Age of Information, first impressions can often take place before you ever meet in person. It's the images, materials, and messages associated with you and your business that speak for you. These include your marketing materials such as business card, logos, website, email address, and others; your social media pages and profiles, updates, and comments; your blog posts and articles; your photographs; and virtually everything else you say, do, or communicate. Any online presence, visual or printed materials, or messages that represent or are attributed to you and your business should be of the utmost quality and align with your desired image as well as your profession, message, and market.

If you wish your potential clients and colleagues to recognize your worth, your business cards or website should be professionally crafted. Certainly there are many do-it-yourself options that will save you money, but use them with care and caution.

try this!

The next time you are having your business cards designed and printed, ask yourself if this will be a card that finds its way into someone's wastebasket. Or will it be a "keeper" that continually reminds the receiver of who you are and the amazing work you do?

Even your email address, emails, and text messages are part of your personal brand. Let's start with the email address – what does it say about you? Is it cryptic or hard to remember? Does it align with who you say you are? Does it say you are a professional, or is it a hold-over from your college days? Use an email address that makes your name and/or your company easy to remember. Ditch any email addresses that may confuse people, erode your credibility, or make it hard for others to remember you.

With all written correspondence, be mindful of the underlying messages you send (or forward) via the frequency, length, nature, and tone of your messages and even words you use. If you want to preserve your image and reputation, don't write or forward anything in any type of written correspondence that you wouldn't want to see written on the front page of a newspaper, plastered on a billboard, or repeated to your grandmother.

Pay attention to your email signature line; this is an often overlooked means of projecting your personality, individuality, and brand. It's basically the signoff at the end of every email and it's automatically added to all of your emails. Many people don't use these or even know they can set them up. At the very least sign off on all your emails with your first and last name (unless you are corresponding with a very close friend or family member). Signature lines should include your title, company name, contact info (as much as you feel comfortable revealing), website URL, and possibly even a statement, tagline or quote that describes you, your company, or one of your key philosophies. Steer away from highly opinionated "bumper sticker" style slogans that may offend.

try this!

Pay attention to the signature lines in the emails you receive. Use these to get ideas for your own. Notice what seems to work, what doesn't and where the balance is between not enough and too much information.

appearance

Your brand is reflected in your appearance, including your grooming, attire, and accessories; your attitude, energy, and demeanor; your body language and posture; and even your facial expressions and your tone of voice.

Your grooming and attire.

Although many current dress codes and trends may indicate the contrary, presenting a professional appearance in the business arena does matter. Casual and comfortable definitely have a stronghold. In fact, casual Fridays have fallen to new depths of casualness. If you're more of a fashionista, it also can be tempting to wear the very latest fashion trends for work (whether they were meant for business or not). In the end, if you want to stand out and make the best possible first impression, dress for business in a way that is age-appropriate and says you are capable, credible, professional, and ready to get to work.

There are even time-tested guidelines as to which specific colors, styles, and details will project the messages and image appropriate for your situation. Moreover, how you dress for one industry may be different from how you dress for another. For example, an attorney or financial planner may dress in a way that is more conservative than a boutique owner, graphic designer, or family therapist. Yet there are universal factors that apply no matter what you do for a living. These include immaculate grooming, including skin, teeth, breath, and nails; a flattering, well-maintained hairstyle and makeup; appropriate professional suits or separates that fit and are clean and pressed; and stylish, appropriate accessories.

There are numerous books and resources that can give you specific tips on what types of attire and accessories are appropriate for your profession. A favorite of mine is *Casual Power: How to Up Your Nonverbal Communication & Dress Down for Success* by Sherry Maysonave.

Sometimes you can do everything right in how you show up and interact with others. But being truly memorable, someone others remember clearly long after an event or interaction is over, is yet another trick.

My friend Karen represents a beautiful line of designer clothing and believes that if you are a quiet and reserved person by nature, it's all the more important to let your wardrobe and accessories help you project more personality and be memorable.

For example, Marlys, a consulting client, is a lovely, kind person with a creative, dynamic background in communications and in championing philanthropy and the arts. She has impeccable manners and good people skills. She is neat, polished, and has excellent follow-through. She shows up one hundred percent wherever she goes. One area where I felt she needed some "oomph" to her brand was in her memorability. She is somewhat soft-spoken and though she dresses well, there was nothing in her style or appearance that really popped." I suggested that she could easily make one small change with her appearance that would more readily reflect her style and creativity. I suggested she wear one piece of stunning, memorable costume jewelry or another accessory such as a purse or scarf that would serve as a conversation piece. This helped Marlys capture attention and start conversations, and also made her more memorable.

try this!

> Engage a professional image consultant. When it comes to honestly seeing and analyzing your current image and brand and improving upon it for maximum impact and results, engaging an objective and well-trained professional can be invaluable. Working with an image professional can be some of the best and most impactful money you will ever invest.

Many image professionals are trained not only in the aesthetics of personal presence, image, and brand, but also in the science and human behavior behind it. They can provide the objectivity, diligence, and tact that friends, family, and colleagues often cannot.

In working with clients, one of the first questions an image consultant may ask a client is how they wish to be perceived. Most people want to exude confidence, intelligence, credibility, approachability, and trustworthiness. And they want to look great and feel confident. Nothing wrong with that!

From here, depending on their training and specialty, a consultant may work with the client on color and style choices that flatter, project the right image, and yet still showcase the client's uniqueness and personality. Many provide personal shopping services.

> Image consulting isn't about fashion. It's about applying socially- and scientifically-based techniques to help you look your best, feel confident, make positive first impressions, and project an image that's in line with what you want to attract.

And please!
No more mug shots or vacation photos!

Your appearance matters in photos too. Every professional worth his or her salt absolutely must have a professional headshot on file. You will use this photo in your promotion and publicity materials; as your avatar on social media; when you write articles or win awards; when you do any public speaking; and to give to the media when asked.

This is not a mug shot taken by your spouse or best friend as you stand in front of a blank wall in your home or office. It is not a cropped photo of you on your wedding day or on vacation. It is not your high school yearbook photo or a photo taken with your pet. It is a photograph taken of you in a studio by a professional photographer with flattering lighting and commercial grade equipment. In this photo you are professionally dressed and coiffed, wearing appropriate makeup, looking your most rested, alert, and polished best. If you already have a great headshot, you know what I'm talking about. If you don't, please get one. You and others will notice the difference.

etiquette

What is etiquette really about? It's not about being 100% "proper" while tipping your nose in the air or maintaining a skyward pinky as you sip your tea delicately out of a china cup. Nor is it about being snooty, better than, or more "proper" than anyone else in the room. Etiquette is about making those around you feel more comfortable, welcomed, appreciated, and at ease.

> Repeat: Business etiquette is not about being better or
> more proper; it's about making those around you feel more
> comfortable, welcomed, appreciated, and at ease.

Replace "hi" with "hello."

International protocol expert Jan Goss advises: the word 'hi' should be stricken from all professional communication and replaced with 'hello.' It is a warmer and more engaging greeting. For an extra touch, add in a second greeting: 'Hello. Good morning.' For the first class treatment, include the person's name, as in 'Hello. Good morning, Sheila.' Doesn't that sound lovely? Try it and see how this makes you feel, but most of all see how others react to it. (Replace "hi" with "hello" when you answer the phone and in your voice mail message, too.)

Make eye contact.

When you are greeting and interacting with someone, look into their eyes. Not in a creepy, no-blinking way, but in an engaged, warm, and respectful way. As fashion photographers will tell you, it's possible to smile with your eyes. The technique is called "smizing." It works. Try it as you converse with others. Relax. Be warm and genuine.

Know how to introduce yourself.

At some point in conversation with a new acquaintance, you will be asked what you do. Here's where you also get to describe who you are, who you serve, and how they benefit. I'm not a fan of the finely crafted, meticulously memorized and stiffly delivered "elevator speech." I believe it's possible for you to introduce yourself and give others a glimpse of what you do naturally and with passion, authenticity, and heart. What's more, you'll want to do so with enough variation so it adapts easily to your audience.

* * *

The basic components of a self introduction are: who you are, what you do, who you serve, and how they benefit.

* * *

No matter the situation, your introduction should be authentic and engaging. You can always improve on it and tweak it. You can do this by taking note of how others react (or not) to what you're saying. Keep tweaking until you land on something that makes others go "aha!"

Here's an example of how I give my introduction, although I will be honest, it varies depending on the conversation and situation, and it never sounds the same way twice.

Hello, my name is Patti DeNucci, I help business people learn how to network with more intention and become more connected and polished so they can attract more powerful relationships, referrals, and results for their businesses. I do this via writing, speaking, consulting, and referral services.

> Important Rule: Never introduce yourself with a complaint,
> self-deprecating statement, or negative story of any kind.
> Don't make others sorry they chose you as a conversation
> partner.

Listen to your voice.

Your voice is definitely a part of who you are and affects your image. This is especially important if your voice is a big part of your profession via presentations, public speaking, webinars, broadcasts, podcasts, or audio books.

What does your voice say about you? That you're young and inexperienced? Tentative? Channeling a Valley Girl? A regular consumer of whiskey and cigars? That you're nervous or anxious? Excited? Stressed? Hopped up on too much caffeine?

Our voices can be trained to sound calm, confident, friendly, and professional. Record and listen to yourself. Ask others what they think. Get coaching if you need it.

I had the pleasure of attending a workshop led by Arthur Samuel Joseph, voice coach to many celebrities and broadcasters and author of *Vocal Power: Harnessing the Power Within*. It was an inspiring day well spent and it opened my eyes to the power of training, developing, and using my voice properly – and practicing what I learned.

Your telephone voice messages are important too. These include both the messages callers hear on your voice mail and the messages you leave for others. Think carefully about these messages as you develop them and record them. If your business line is also your personal home line, please resist the urge to create cutesy voice mail or answering machine messages. And, while adorable and witty, it's certainly not appropriate to have your child or dog be the voice of the message. Instead try something simple such as, "Hello, this is Jane. I am unable to take your call at the moment. Please leave me a message and your phone number so I can return your call."

your unique energy, attitude, and "vibe"

There is nothing so powerful and attractive as the person who can generate, maintain, and exude a steady flow of positive energy and a genuinely confident, upbeat attitude. The British journalist and amateur historian Harold Wilkins noted that, "The world of achievement has always belonged to the optimist." This is so true.

While attending a national conference I decided to conduct a casual experiment. I became hyper-aware of the people I encountered and the kind of energy they gave off. I'm happy to report that most of the people I interacted with gave off positive "vibes." They smiled, laughed, and had sparkle in their eyes. They were alert, walked and sat tall, and showed up with purpose. They made others around them, including me, feel good.

Likewise, I made note of the few people who brought me down. These individuals wore scowls or blank stares and had closed, defensive, tired, or even timid body language. I was aware of comments that were whiny or negative. I couldn't wait to get out of the range of these energy depleters. Their tired, stressed, uncertain energy was contagious. I wanted none of it!

There is much to say and many books written about human behavior, moods, energy fields, mirror neurons, vibes, and the laws of positive attraction. It's been proven that one person's mood can affect that of everyone in the vicinity. I'll leave those discussions to the experts, but as these pertain to your personal brand and image and your ability to attract what you want, here are a few guidelines to help ensure that you give off positive energy regularly:

- ⁜ Understand that you are in control of your own happiness and mood.

- ⁜ Do what brings you energy and joy – it will help energize you.

- ⁜ Leverage your strengths as opposed to fighting your weaknesses.

- ⁜ Be clear on your vision, intentions, and goals.

- ⁜ Avoid negative people.

- ⁜ Avoid gossip and gossipy people.

- ⁜ Practice forgiveness.

- ⁜ Let go of what's not working; seek and connect with what does.

- ⁜ Consider who else is in the vicinity and how you are affecting them.

you are known by the quality of your character

Good character and unshakable integrity are traits that are measured by actions over time. If you have character and integrity, you reveal in your everyday actions that you are honest, authentic, and genuine as well as caring, committed, and dependable. You are interested in and committed to doing the right thing. You consistently model high moral standards and use these to guide you as you make positive and productive choices. You are not about winning or succeeding unless you can do so honorably. You show emotional intelligence and humility. (According to a definition given me by my colleague Nancy Oelklaus, Ed. D., author of *Journey from Head to Heart: Living and Working Authentically,* "humility is being no *more* but also no less than who you truly are.") You are optimistic, supportive, and respectful of others. You want the best for them, not just for you.

Character, kindness, and integrity are important to Tony Hsieh, CEO of Zappos.com and author of *Delivering Happiness: A Path to Profits, Passion, and Purpose.* When Tony speaks in public, he shares stories about his company's hiring practices as they search for people who demonstrate the characteristic that will reinforce the Zappos brand: delivering happiness. Among these stories, he speaks of what happens when the company flies candidates in for interviews. The first question the interviewer asks about the candidate is not even directed to the candidate. It's directed at the airport shuttle driver: "How did this person treat you?" If the driver reports that the candidate was in any way rude, mean, disengaged, or disrespectful, the interview is over before it begins. The candidate is sent home on the spot as he or she does not reflect the company's philosophies about human interaction. What a simple but effective test!

Sincerity relates to your authenticity as well. When you are sincere, you are engaged, honest, and open. When you are authentic, you are who you are and are not pretending to be someone or something you are not. You are being your best *true* self. Although there is some wisdom in the "fake it 'til you make it" theory, trying to be someone you're not as a regular habit is a form of dishonesty. Others will figure you out eventually and you'll lose credibility and trust.

* * *

You never know who else may be watching, listening, and taking in a first impression and getting a glimpse of your brand.

* * *

Just as a chain is only as strong as its weakest link, your personality, image, and brand are only as strong and memorable as your consistency in showing and demonstrating them to others. Ask yourself if you show up in a consistent, sustainable manner every day. Or perhaps you are "up" one day and "down" the next? Do people wonder which "you" will show up on any given day? Consider that neither unpredictability nor volatility are attractive.

If you look around you, you'll see that people who are successful and attractive to others continually seek excellence, and strive to make improvements in everything they do. They also face their fears. It's how they stretch and grow. This takes vision, courage, and determination. It is the mark of a leader. Do you seek to present and provide your absolute best to others every day? Do you consistently seek out and try to offer excellence? Do you regularly try to improve your standards? Even when it gets uncomfortable or scary?

* * *

Consider the Law of Attraction: you are most likely to get what you think about, focus on, and project to others.

* * *

emotional intelligence or EQ

According to experts, EQ is the ability to be in control of yourself and your emotions, even under stress. I like to say it's the art of acting like a grown-up. It's your "street smarts." EQ is how you:

- ❋ **understand and express yourself.**

- ❋ **understand and relate to others.**

- ❋ **get along in the world.**

- ❋ **take care of yourself and manage your life.**

- ✳ respond to change and stress.

- ✳ solve problems.

- ✳ generate positive moods.

- ✳ self-motivate when setting and achieving goals.

- ✳ improvise, adapt, and overcome challenges.

Knowing this, I'm glad I had the experience of being a Girl Scout when I was a girl, This organization understood EQ before it was even called EQ. The Girl Scout Pledge illustrates this beautifully. Here's how it goes today: "I will do my best to be honest and fair, friendly and helpful, considerate and caring, courageous and strong, and responsible for what I say and do. And to respect myself and others, respect authority, use resources wisely, make the world a better place, and be a sister to every Girl Scout."

One of my son's soccer coaches, Peter Dolan, has his own version of this pledge. It goes like this: "Be ready. No whining."

your brand and image extends beyond you

Your brand is pervasive. It reaches into the territory inhabited by those who influence you most, and who you, in turn, influence. Whoever and whatever is contained in this territory reflects on you. Your brand is reflected in the company you keep, including:

- ✳ **Your circle of friends.**

- ✳ **The people in your address book or database.**

- ✳ **Your memberships, associations, and affiliations.**

- ✳ **Your clients, colleagues, and affiliates.**

* ❋ **Your social media lists – who you follow, who follows you.**

* ❋ **Your recommendations and referrals.**

* ❋ **The causes you support.**

* ❋ **The businesses and establishments you frequent.**

You also reflect on them. I grew up in a small town and was constantly reminded of this from an early age. Not only did my parents want me to create and preserve a good image, reputation for myself, they were also very aware of how my actions, choices, image, and reputation would affect our family's reputation. They regularly reminded me of this. My dad was a business owner who worked hard to earn customers and their trust. My behavior or that of my siblings would reflect on our family and Dad's business. In turn, it could also affect his employees and their families. We were all interconnected. So are you.

> Consider the ripples that occur when you choose to show up and be your best self to the world. Or not. It's not just about you, it's also about your business, clients, family, friends, mentors, and colleagues.

weaknesses and blind spots: we all have them

It can be satisfying to discover, understand, and leverage your talents, strengths, and preferences, but realizing that you, as a mere mortal, have your own unique set of weaknesses and blind spots is critical as well. Like the rest of us, you are human and imperfect. You have your good days and your not-so-good days. You do some things very well, but you also may not be the best at handling certain tasks and situations. You could be making mistakes that are obvious to others, but are completely out of your range of vision (hence the term blind spot) or in that place we hate to admit we have: "The Denial Zone."

It can be worthwhile to acknowledge and make friends with your flaws and imperfections. After all, pretending to be perfect is ridiculous and exhausting. And it usually backfires, alienates others, and prevents you from seeing the truth, learning, and improving.

Blind spots can hurt both individuals and businesses. I know of a well-established, upscale boutique that was facing increased competition, but chose not to invest in basic customer service training for the young and inexperienced staff it hired. (The owner didn't want to spend the money.) I experienced the negative side effect of that decision one day. I entered the store ready to invest in some new pieces for my professional wardrobe. I was ready to buy, but unfortunately I was ignored by, not just one, but *all* of the gum-chewing, self-absorbed salesclerks stationed on the sales floor. They weren't busy with other customers, just busy talking to each other and clueless as to my existence. After perusing several departments, I walked out and never went back. One employee did bother to say "Ba-bye." You can say that again. That was the last time I ever went to that store. Within two months the store announced its closing. Not a surprise.

Resist resistance and skepticism.

As shown by the story at the beginning of this chapter, people frequently resist upgrading their personal image and branding. They often do not take it seriously, or believe it is an unnecessary luxury. They:

- ❋ **are in denial and don't see how their current appearance, image, communications, and brand are detracting from their success.**

* think the whole notion of personal image is fluffy and ridiculous.

* insist they should be judged according to their abilities, track record, education, and who they are on the inside.

* believe that feedback from friends and family is enough (besides it's cheaper) and balk at bringing in trained and objective experts.

* don't understand the psychology behind personal brand.

* believe they already know how to create their brand.

* put it off and wait for the perfect time (such as when they've lost weight or made more money).

* don't feel they deserve this much help or attention.

* fear change and prefer their current level of discomfort.

* are unwilling to invest in this "soft" area, but do so in the "hard" areas of technology or marketing.

* believe that other people should accept them as they are.

This is inaccurate thinking that stands in the way of success. The bottom line is: if you want to project a polished, credible, and memorable personal brand that aligns with your intentions and goals and helps you achieve the success you deserve, you must be open to investing in yourself, hearing the objective truth, and making some critical changes that will help your "personal packaging" align with your talents, credibility, experience, and strengths.

try this!

Ask yourself what five words you believe others would use to describe you, as a friend, a colleague, or a business person. Then ask several friends, colleagues, or even people you've just met to choose five words to describe how they perceive you. How do these align? Do you see parallels and consistency, or disparity?

* * *

When you ask for honest and constructive feedback from people, be grateful, open, and willing to hear the truth and act on it. Even if it stings, this is how you will get better.

* * *

why do this work?

To answer this question, let me ask you another one. Your Next Big Opportunity may be right in front of you – are you ready? I'm often surprised at how casually people dress and how ill-prepared they are when they attend professional meetings and networking events. Many show up looking like they just threw on whatever outfit was closest at hand. In addition, they appear to have given little thought to the mood they are projecting, lack many basic social skills, and offer limp, non-enthusiastic handshakes. They forget to bring their business cards, and if you ask if they can send you a copy of their resume or CV they look at you as if you've lost your mind. Yet they have invested in the time and money it takes to attend and participate in these meetings. Some may even be leaders of organizations. I can't understand why they do this. What are they thinking they will attract?

One day, as I was speaking to a group of entrepreneurs and consultants, I decided to make a point about this. The topic of my speech had to do with attracting and developing more clients and referrals.

As usual, I was shocked at how casually many of the attendees were dressed for this event, particularly given the topic. Some were wearing shorts and sandals. Others looked like they had just rolled out of bed or were taking a break from mowing the lawn, cleaning the garage, or grooming the dog.

Halfway through my talk, when I was speaking on how critical it is to make positive and professional first impressions, I mentioned that I had arranged a surprise for the group: some colleagues who were looking for experts and suppliers to work with them on some very lucrative projects would be joining us after the meeting to do some on-the-spot interviews. The looks on some of the faces indicated I had struck a nerve.

"You're ready, here and now, to do an interview and make a great first impression?" I asked the group. "Right?"

Silence. Many of the attendees squirmed in their chairs. No, unfortunately most of them were not ready. One person even piped up and said, "No one told us about this."

Well of course not. Sometimes the best opportunities and the most important people in your professional world will arrive unannounced!

To the audience's relief I admitted there was no colleague coming, nor would there be any interviews.

"But *why* aren't you ready?" I asked. "Isn't this meeting – really *every* meeting, *every* coffee appointment or lunch date, and even every encounter and every trip outside the walls of your office or home a potential opportunity to meet people, make connections, showcase your best self, mention what you do professionally, and potentially win an opportunity or earn a referral?"

* * *

Why would you not want to be ready and at your very best, should your Next Big Break show up in the next few moments?

* * *

Some of the people in my audience got it. Others, unfortunately, will continue to fight this because they still believe that they should only be judged for what's inside. They don't want to "sell out."

What about you? Are you ready to exude the intentional image and brand that will help you attract what you want and deserve?

❋ focus on quality

IT'S NOT ABOUT HOW MANY CONNECTIONS YOU HAVE

In this chapter, you will:

- Learn how and why to shift your focus from quantity to quality.

- Analyze what and who really bring you the results you want.

- Discover how to have more time for what matters most to you.

focus on quality | 77

In planning for the coming year, Ethan worked on creating a weekly scheduling template. He was particularly interested in seeing how much time he should set aside for coffee and lunch dates, networking luncheons, and other social, professional, and business development events. He glanced with satisfaction at his large database of contacts, which included a huge array of friends, colleagues, clients, possible venture partners, referral sources, advisors, vendors, professional contacts, prospects, and others – almost everyone from whom he had received a business card in the last five years. In addition, Ethan had a stack of business cards he'd accumulated from recent networking events. These were new contacts he wanted to know better, many of whom had invited him to meet and visit over coffee or lunch. Ethan felt extremely popular!

A devoted networker and a firm believer in the power of connections, Ethan enjoyed building relationships. He was a people person and most of his business came from referrals. But as he did some quick math he experienced a paradigm shift.

Ethan noted that he typically worked forty-eight weeks out of the year and devoted an average of forty to forty-five hours a week to his business activities, including time with clients, marketing activities, and administrative projects. This schedule gave him time for some writing, his family, and training for a triathlon, which was a passion for him.

As Ethan made his calculations, he discovered that if he hoped to have even one phone chat, coffee, or lunch with each contact in his database plus attend one or two networking or association events a week, he'd be spending *all* of his working hours on the phone, at coffee, at lunch, or out of the office. It was clear he'd need to double the hours in his work week if he had any chance of keeping up with his networking schedule, handling projects from his existing list of clients and tending to other business tasks.

This was not acceptable to Ethan. He did not want to give up the time with his kids, his writing, or his athletic training. Additionally, he was not in a position to add more staff or expand his marketing budget.

The light went on for Ethan. He realized he needed to become more focused and selective concerning where he invested his energies and time. He realized that he must figure out which clients, contacts, networking efforts, professional memberships, and commitments created the most profitable and satisfying results and value for him and his business. To do that, he needed to know what characteristics these valuable contacts shared, and how to focus on and attract them and only them.

Ethan's planning suddenly addressed different issues, such as how to focus his time, energy, and resources, and how to develop a method that would help him become more discerning and disciplined. He saw that there could be a downside to having too many contacts in his database, which had actually grown too large to manage. He had reached his CCM (Connections Critical Mass). It was suddenly clear to him that more is not always better.

Like other enthusiastic networkers and extroverts, Ethan had believed everyone he met and every business function he attended had something to offer him and his business. His open-ended, open-minded approach may have been a great way to take his first steps when his business was young and his database small, but things were different now. As his business matured and his database and networking calendar grew, they were on the verge of robbing him and his business of valuable time, resources, and energy.

Ethan's phone was ringing and his email inbox was always full. Both of these situations could be perceived as signs of a healthy business. However, more and more of these calls and emails were just "connections clutter": invitations to sales events and fundraisers from people he hardly knew, requests to have lunch or coffee from contacts who wanted his time, energy, or advice (usually for free), requests from prospects who desired his services and expertise, but had K-Mart budgets or could only pay him on spec. Ethan was also being invited to serve on committees, write and contribute articles, and speak at or emcee events. Some of these were potentially excellent opportunities, but many were requests for Ethan's time and expertise, often without any compensation.

It was all becoming overwhelming. Things had to change.

Note this wasn't about Ethan becoming a snob or acting like he was better than anyone else. It simply meant it was time for him to move to another level of discipline and focus. He finally saw that as a small business owner he had a finite amount of time to work and connect.

analyze who and what is right for you and your business

Does Ethan's story sound familiar? If you're like Ethan and find yourself swamped by an unwieldy database, an overactive networking schedule, and an increased demand for your time and expertise without sufficient return or compensation, here are some steps you can take to become more focused on quality and results. The methods described here are a great way to reach greater clarity on what feeds you and your business so you can:

⁎ **focus.**

⁎ **invest your time, energy, and resources wisely.**

* attract and build worthwhile relationships.

* move to a new level of efficiency, productivity, and results.

Start with the 80:20 Rule.

Also known as the Pareto Principle, the 80:20 Rule states that typically 80% of most results come from 20% of the causes. For example, you probably wear 20% of the clothes in your closet 80% of the time. Or you may use 20% of the ingredients in your cupboard, pantry, or refrigerator in 80% of your meals. And you probably spend 80% of your time with 20% of your friends.

You can apply the 80:20 Rule in a multitude of ways to figure out what quality means to you and your business. Ask yourself:

Which 20% of your

* **Clients**

* **Contacts**

* **Friendships**

* **Associations/Memberships**

* **Networking events**

* **Coffees/Lunches**

Bring you 80% of your

* **Profits, most rewarding projects, and testimonials**

* **Referrals, ideas, tips, news, and valuable opportunities**

* **Clients, connections, and news on best practices**

* **Enjoyment, energy, inspiration, and support**

Put the 80:20 Rule to use in as many ways to analyze as many situations as you can think of. You will gain a profound new perspective on the value of just about every relationship you have and every activity into which you put time, energy, and resources. From there, you can learn to recognize the traits of the people and opportunities that have the highest potential to be your Top Customers and Contacts (a.k.a. Twenty Percenters or Top 20%) from the get-go. This will enable you to energize yourself and your business rather than to deplete it.

> When you can create an efficient goldmine of a database
> and a more focused networking schedule, that's the basis for
> intentional networking.

It's not always about money.

I have several colleagues who are not clients of mine, nor am I a client of theirs. Money is neither mentioned nor exchanged except when we are debating whose turn it is to pick up the lunch tab. Yet we exchange priceless information and solve many business dilemmas when we put our heads together. We are each other's loyal and trusting advisors. People like this can be among your most valuable business allies and assets, so don't discount them just because you didn't make a monetary profit from your association with them.

Likewise, treasure your best, most encouraging friends. They may fit into your top 20% because you simply enjoy being around them. You sparkle in their presence. You pick up the phone when you see their number on caller ID and are always eager to see them, They inspire and energize you. They support and appreciate you and find every opportunity to let you know it. They give you honest feedback when you need a fresh perspective. There is value in this level of friendship. Through thick and thin, we all need these close relationships to keep going.

It's also important to feel the satisfaction of giving back. Giving to others can bring you value if you choose your pro bono projects, volunteer commitments, and leadership contributions wisely. For example, you may find it energizing to mentor someone who is eager to hear and act on your guidance; someone who you can watch blossom into an amazing leader. And it may be worthwhile on many levels to volunteer your time to a professional association or non-profit organization or to speak pro bono before a group. You can learn new skills and demonstrate those you already have. There can be plenty of value here.

define and document the profile of your top 20%

Now that you have an idea as to the Top 20% in your database who bring you 80% of your business or other positive results, it's time to figure out what qualities or characteristics these high-value, high-performing clients, contacts, advisors, friends, events, commitments, and appointments share. You may note some patterns here as well.

This is an important step as it helps you define and identify what "quality" means to you and your business. It also will make it easier for you to tune your "radar" to spotting certain traits in people and events down the road, thus helping you recognize potential Twenty Percenters more readily if and when you're ready to seek more of them.

Analyze the connection.

How, where, and under what circumstances did you initially connect with the person or opportunity? Did they meet you as a result of a talk you gave at a luncheon or an article you wrote for the local business journal? Did you meet on an airplane or at a workshop or cocktail party? Did someone refer or introduce you or somehow create the circumstances of your meeting? The more you can remember and record about how you met the better.

For example, let's say Mary Jones is your best client. You met her through your colleague John Anderson. You and John used to work together at Company XYZ. You heard about your job at Company XYZ via Ann Smith who you met at a networking event given by an association you belong to. You get the idea.

Dig down into the layers of circumstances, names, places, and events that brought you your best clients, colleagues, and opportunities. Document them; they hold clues as to who and what works best to bring you the most fortunate contacts, connections, and circumstances.

Describe the characteristics of your Top 20%.

Come up with descriptive words and phrases to describe the characteristics of your most valuable clients and contacts. These words and phrases help you define what you are attracted to, what "quality" means for you, and ultimately what results in good fortune for you and your business. Add as many notes or traits as you can think of. You can devote an entire notebook or file to your list of traits and notes about your favorite people, clients, and opportunities. You will start to notice patterns that reveal what quality and value mean to you. This new awareness will make it much easier for you to recognize what fits into your world and what doesn't, which is equally valuable.

Develop your unique set of criteria.

Come up with a list of questions to ask yourself about people, situations, and events, as well as how you make decisions about them.

These can further help you document the characteristics valuable in your work and life. The more yes answers you get, the more likely you have a fit. Here are some examples:

Does this person/organization/product/service/event/resource:

- ❋ **Bring something positive and worthwhile to you or your organization in terms of revenue, referrals, support, expertise, energy, or enjoyment?**

- ❋ **Value, align with, or in some way compliment your expertise, time, and skills?**

- ❋ **Reflect well on you and your organization?**

- ❋ **Believe in and actively support "win-win" situations?**

- ❋ **Follow a code or set of values that align with yours?**

- ❋ **Participate in the ebb and flow and development of the relationship?**

- ❋ **Help you propel your business, projects, dreams, and goals forward?**

try this!

Apply "The Energy Test." This is an elegantly simple way to measure who or what is a good fit for you. Simply note how you feel after you've interacted with a person or client, attended an event, participated in a program, served on a board, or spent time on a project. Was the experience energizing, depleting, or neither? Make a note about this on your calendar or schedule or list the interactions in a notebook. Use a plus (+) for the energizers, a zero (0) for the so-sos, and a minus (-) for the negatives. Strive for nothing less than all "+'s."

Sure, no relationship is perfect and no client, project, group, event, or commitment is always going to be energizing, but you'll quickly begin to see patterns. Use this information to make decisions on whether or not to schedule or attract more of the same.

And remember that everything is subject to change. What was once energizing may no longer be so. Check in with your feelings, attitude, and energy levels. Make adjustments accordingly.

create your top contact list

When you become aware of and accustomed to evaluating who and what is best for you and your business, take a next step that further refines your Top 20%: create a list of your Top 10, 25, 50, or even 100 or 150 contacts, clients, projects, colleagues, associations, or obligations. These can further whittle down where you want to devote the majority of your time and energy.

Just like the clothing items that are the favorites in your wardrobe, these are your favorites in your database. They are your Inner Circle or even your Board of Advisors. Who would you put on this list, and why? Understand that the list will probably evolve over time. Create systems for keeping actively in touch and engaged with these.

Consider having two databases.

One database is reserved for only your most valuable clients and contacts. Another list is for everyone else. This works well for businesses that host events such as workshops or teleseminars, or sell products such as books, workbooks, CDs, DVDs, and other items. For these lists, quantity is important.

An alternative is to stick with one database, but use filters. If you want to keep only one database, be sure it has the capability to help you categorize and filter so you can readily identify your Top 20% when you need to.

Though you will focus on your Top 20%, devoting time for meetings, calls, and personal notes, find and implement creative ways to stay in touch with the masses. Efficient ways to stay in touch with many people can be found using email and social media. Use these thoughtfully and strategically.

> Focusing on your Top 20% is not about being elitist; it's about focusing on what is right for you and what helps you stay energized and feel "fed" so you can continue to be productive and create the best results for you and your business.

why do this work?

As you become a seeker of quality, you and your brand become associated with quality. Why? Because your choices and associations reflect who you are, what you're all about, what's important to you, and what you want. You gain credibility for your focus, authenticity, judiciousness, and integrity. You demonstrate that you are selective, and that you have high standards. Others notice this and the ones who matter will appreciate it.

For example, I know that my friend Renée Trudeau, a life coach and author, is extremely protective of her time and resources, very selective about anyone she works with, and makes all choices deliberately. Therefore when I ask her for a recommendation or when she sends someone my way, I know she has given it a lot of thought and care. Ninety-nine percent of the time she is spot-on and I enjoy great experiences and results. I trust her and hold her opinions in high esteem. Talk about power and influence!

Being selective is an indicator that you are purposeful, serious about quality, and exercise good judgment. It helps solidify your reputation, builds trust, and brings you increased power to attract more good people – and even more good fortune. Smart successful people generally want to do business with other smart and successful people.

* * *

As you become more intentional, you will likely discover that some people and activities are no longer a fit for you; you can no longer expend energy on them. That is part of growth and change, for them and for you.

* * *

As a final note, always hold yourself to the same high standards you set for others. As you analyze what you want and need, don't forget to do some self-examination as well. Regularly and honestly consider whether you are living up to the high standards to which you are holding others. What are you doing to create relationships that are mutually beneficial?

What are you doing to earn your spot in the Top 20% of those you work with, admire, and receive value from?

Are you a Twenty-Percenter with your 20%? This is a key component to being in integrity with yourself and others. As you scrutinize others, expect that they will do the same with you.

✳ say no with grace

SETTING LIMITS, BOUNDARIES, AND POLICIES

In this chapter, you will:

- Learn how and when to say no to projects, requests, and events that don't align with your mission and purpose.

- See the benefits of clearing your calendar and database of unnecessary clutter.

- Discover how to deal with interruptions and distractions, brain-pickers, and other productivity killers.

- Find that sweet spot that allows you to be helpful and supportive to others, while remaining true to your own desires, needs, and goals.

Pamela was stressed, drained, and frustrated. Three big responsibilities had stretched her to capacity: dealing with the daily demands of being a parent; running a growing consulting practice; and serving on the board of a professional association.

After suffering a case of the flu that nearly turned into pneumonia and discovering that her end-of-year numbers were not where they should be for the third year in a row, Pamela knew it was time to take corrective action. First, she had to start taking better care of herself. Second, she wanted more time with her husband and children as well as some time for her close friends and hobbies. Third, she needed greater efficiency and profitability in her business and wanted to leverage her growing reputation. To honor these needs and goals, Pamela knew it was time to rid herself of anything draining her energy, wasting her time, diluting her focus, creating stress, and costing her valuable relationships and revenue.

Pamela made a list of priorities and began assessing every part of her life and work. She started to pay attention to how many requests, interruptions, and distractions flew at her each day – and how she was dealing with them. After just one week she saw clear patterns. "I found myself saying yes to things that weren't in line with what I wanted, and I allowed far too many interruptions and distractions to destroy my focus," says Pamela. "I love what I do, I have a lot of friends and colleagues, I love helping others, and I want everyone to know how capable I am. But I was doing too much for too many people, giving too much away, and not holding true to my own needs, goals, and boundaries. Basically, I had set myself up as an easy target."

Pamela admits that it was through her own choices that her life and business were spinning out of control. "The truth is, I had taught others that it was okay to take advantage of me, my time, and my expertise. If I didn't make changes I was sure it would cost me my health, my sanity, precious time with my family, my most valuable colleagues, and my business."

True success demands focus and discipline

A mentor shared this wisdom with me several years ago when I too was feeling overwhelmed with requests: "However much you are willing to give, others will be more than happy to take. And they will keep taking as long as you keep giving." She wasn't necessarily telling me to stop giving, but to give with greater care and intention.

One thing is clear: if you want to stay focused on your vision, intentions, goals, and needs, if you want to uphold your image and brand, and if you are serious about focusing on quality over quantity, you must learn to set clear limits and boundaries. You must know how and when to graciously say "no thank you." It's just part of the deal.

> I once heard a story illustrating the power of focus. At a business luncheon, the speaker compared a 40-watt laser beam with a 40-watt incandescent bulb. He noted that both use the same amount of power: 40 watts. However, the incandescent bulb disperses soft light all around while the laser beam has a much more powerful, pinpoint focus. The incandescent bulb barely illuminates a closet; the laser can cut through steel. Which are you? Which would you rather be?

How and where you choose to spend your time, energy, resources, and expertise will always have a cost, whether it supports your needs and desires or not. When you choose to say yes to one request, you are inevitably bound to say no to something else. You can try to override this law to some extent, but eventually burnout, broken promises, stress, illness, lost business, and other negative results will show up.

So how and where are you choosing to spend your time, attention, energy, and resources? How are these choices affecting your life and work? It is worthwhile to become aware of everyone and everything that's tugging at you. Examine habits and attitudes that may be holding you back.

In his book *The Big Leap*, Gay Hendricks talks about the many attitudes, habits, situations, and relationships that can create what he calls "Upper Limit Problems" for us when we are on the road to success. These are the little (and sometimes big) things we do to self-sabotage our success, often subconsciously. What creates obstacles and Upper Limit Problems for you? Trying to do too much for too many people without sufficient exchange could be one of them. You can't fix, change, or delete all roadblocks and stress-inducing habits overnight, but you can begin to be aware of them and delete the ones that are easy to change or let go of first.

Let's say your sweet and loyal, but needy friend Jessie calls you every Monday morning, usually interrupting your weekly strategizing time. Her purpose is to "check in on you" but you've noticed she does most of the talking, filling you in on all the drama that occurred in her world over the weekend. This conversation usually takes, at minimum, fifteen minutes. You want to be a supportive friend, but listening to your friend's endless list of problems, calamities, and relationship woes leaves you feeling drained and distracted. Somehow you've chosen to let this weekly tradition continue, at the expense of your important planning session.

You're just getting back to the task at hand, when your job-hunting colleague Betty calls (for the fourth time in as many weeks) to ask you for feedback on her latest resume revision. You patiently read the file she emails and provide her with feedback (on the spot and free of charge, even though you offer this service as part of your business). The call finally ends after you've answered several of Betty's questions. You look at your watch and realize you've been on the phone with her for more than forty-five minutes. You also realize you have to leave soon for a lunch appointment with someone you met at a networking event. At this point you wish you could cancel because you have so much on your plate, you've already lost the morning and your energy, and you are fairly certain this person will probably wheedle you into some free advice or drop an unwanted sales pitch on you.

By now you're mentally exhausted, completely unmotivated and unproductive, and have lost the energy flow you brought with you to the office. Another Monday morning down the drain. Sigh.

> It may sound selfish to begrudge requests for help from friends, colleagues, and contacts, but the truth is, endlessly giving just because you have not set up some reasonable boundaries and don't know how to say no, can create burnout and bitterness, delay your own projects, and compromise your customer service. Ultimately it may even cost you your business. Or your health.

You have the power to preserve your time, energy, and resources for what matters to you. You can summon that power, hone it, and put it to good use.

boundaries and policies

Boundaries

Boundaries help you define and uphold what is important to you and what is not. Like a moat that's put around a castle for protection, boundaries allow you to protect what's yours, including your energy, time, focus, attention, resources, and even your state of mind.

Right now I have firm boundaries set around this day as I work. I'm not checking or responding to email. I'm not answering the phone unless it's a call from my husband or son. I've taken the dog on an extra long, sensory-stimulating walk this morning so she's content to snooze in her chair for the rest of the day. I've pulled up the virtual drawbridge for the next few hours.

Sometimes you have to get this specific and fiercely protective in your life and work, particularly when you have demands on your time, deadlines to meet, or have achieved things that others may want to take from you, be it money, connections, expertise, or some other tangible or intangible asset. You can even be the victim of emotional hijacking, where someone tries to unload their stress, troubles or challenges onto you, usually just when you're enjoying a great day. You do have the right to protect what's yours and decide where the boundaries lie, even if they change each day.

Policies

Similar to boundaries, policies are wonderful things to adopt in your life, particularly if you are continually tapped for help, time, attention, energy, resources, advice, money, or favors – anything that takes you away from your vision, intentions, goals, and action items. In her blog "Women, Clarity & Power", Dr. Ann Daly notes, "Companies have policies. Why can't individuals have policies? In essence, a policy is another conscious boundary we set in order to ensure that we're operating at our best at all times."

Here's how to set some policies for yourself: think about your work and your life and notice situations that make you stressed, uncomfortable, or bitter. For example, you are tired of your friend assuming you will tend to her ornery cat while she goes off on vacation for the fifth time in the last three months. Or you have grown weary of a certain person borrowing books from your business library and not returning them promptly. Or you really don't appreciate how many people call you at work and ask you out to coffee so they can pick your brain until your eye sockets are deep, black, bat-infested caves.

Time to set a policy! This sets up, in advance, what you are and are not willing to do. So when the situation arises, you don't have to stammer, stall, and think something up on the fly (or worse, give in to their request). You already have your firm, well thought-out policy in place. Furthermore, it's not a decision that's directed at anyone in particular; therefore they can't take it personally. And if they try to take it personally, you can say, "Oh, I'm so sorry, but it's my *policy*."

> Policies are essentially decisions made objectively and in advance to prevent problems, confusion, or discomfort, and to bring more focus, ease, and efficiency to your life and work. If you don't have some in place, it's time you did.

For example, you can create the policy that you are no longer a volunteer pet sitter. Never. Not for anyone. Now it's a pre-made decision. It's already made! It's a *policy*. You get the idea.

how and why to say yes — and no

Become aware of how often you say yes – and why. If you're like a lot of people, you probably say yes to requests or opportunities you didn't want, didn't ask for, are not your responsibility, are not necessary or important, or are not helpful to you or to your work. It's time to ask yourself why you say yes. Is it to be nice, agreeable, helpful, or part of the crowd? Is it to alleviate possible guilt? Could it be you have an overdeveloped sense of responsibility or a need to control? Does it make you feel more capable or powerful? Maybe you find yourself saying yes impulsively, without thinking. You're just flowing along in the moment. It's just a habit.

Saying yes can be a good thing; it can be the portal that leads you into amazing new opportunities or relationships. Sometimes it's your duty to say yes. And sometimes it's just the right thing to say. The point here is to be more mindful and strategic as to *why* and *when* you say yes; to have in place some guidelines and policies.

> If you are clear and mindful on who you are, what matters to you, and what you're trying to accomplish in your life and work, you can begin to say yes to that which supports those choices and moves you forward. Additionally, you will know exactly when to say a gracious, but firm "no thank you."

Like many things in life, it comes down to balance. I try to balance 50:50 between being purposeful and mindful, and allowing synchronicity to exert its power (based on my visions and intentions, of course). I also try to maintain the fine balance between serving others and honoring my own needs and vision. Your balance may vary according to your situation, needs, and preferences.

Learn why, when, and how to say "no thank you."

It's quite simple: become more mindful and assertive about saying "no thank you" to requests, offers, and opportunities that don't align with who you are; your values and priorities; your mission and purpose; your vision, intentions, and goals; the image and brand you wish to project; and your dedication to quality over quantity. The strength and discipline to say no to something that does not align with these factors will open up the time, resources, and energy that allow you to say yes to something that is. Consider saying "no thank you" when requests, offers, and opportunities:

- ❋ **Are not the best uses of your time, talents, or resources.**

- ❋ **Don't propel you forward toward your purpose, mission, vision, or goals.**

- ❋ **Don't feed your purpose and passion.**

- ❋ **Cause you to neglect or compromise something important to you, such as your health or family.**

- ❋ **Could negatively affect your reputation.**

- ❋ **Don't feel "right" in your heart or gut.**

- ❋ **Don't interest, inspire, feed, or energize you.**

- ❋ **Create resentment.**

- ❋ **Could create unwanted attention or "noise."**

- ❋ **Should be handled by someone else.**

- ❋ **Don't need to be handled at all.**

- ❋ **Are professional requests that should require scheduling and compensation.**

It can be hard to say no, but to stay true to what's right for you, it's a necessary part of life. There are gracious ways to do it: stand tall, say it like you mean it, keep it short and sweet, and hold fast. No waffling. If you hesitate, you could be persuaded to say yes out of guilt or weakness.

My favorite ways to say no are:

- ☼ **No, thank you.**

- ☼ **No, not today.**

- ☼ **No, that doesn't work for me.**

- ☼ **No, that's not a fit for me.**

- ☼ **No, I can't help you with that.**

- ☼ **No, I'm not available.**

- ☼ **No, I have another commitment.**

- ☼ **No, but I'm confident you can figure that out.**

- ☼ **No, I just can't say yes to that.**

- ☼ **No, I can't do this, but I can do this: _____.**

try this!

Sometimes it may not be obvious whether you should say yes or no. In that case, here are some decision-making tips that might help: vow not to make decisions on the fly. Instead, try these:

- Simply say, "I'll need to think about that and get back to you later."

- Incorporate the Overnight Test (a.k.a. sleep on it) or request longer to decide if needed.

- Check in with your head, your heart, and your gut.

- Meditate or pray about it and see what answer comes up.

- Imagine yourself saying yes. How does this feel?

- Imagine you've said no. How does this feel?

- Go with the decision that leaves you with the more positive feeling a day later.

- When you find yourself having to say yes to something that you'd rather say no to, find a way to negotiate for something that makes it more agreeable or valuable to you.

- Or try saying this: "I'm just not ready to make that decision right now."

Sometimes you might feel exceptionally overworked, overwhelmed, or stressed. This is a good time to make a policy to say no to every request, unless it's something that will energize or restore you. Don't feel guilty. It's your policy, remember?

> You said yes and then realized you should have said no. Now what? Broken promises damage reputations quickly. This dilemma will teach you quickly that a no up-front is better than saying yes and having to back out. If you can follow through with your yes with relative ease, by all means do so. If you simply cannot, be honest about it, apologize profusely, and at the very least try to find an alternative solution.

Use your heart as well as your head.

Michelann Quimby, an organizational leadership expert, notes that it's important to be completely aware of your mind, body, and emotions when making decisions, particularly requests that come from other people. Your heart and emotions may warm up to the person who uses charm, compliments, and flattery, but your intellect may catch an inconsistency or incongruity between the other person's speech and action. This could raise a yellow flag telling you to hesitate or exercise caution. Here's a list of techniques others may use to get you to say yes:

* **Flattery**

* **Charm**

* **Compliments**

* **Threats**

* **Guilt**

* **Exaggeration**

* **Scare tactics**

* **Sympathy**

* **Drama (real or imagined)**

* **Manipulation**

* **Time limits**

* **Scarcity**

* **Pity**

* **Catching you off guard or in a weak moment**

* **Putting you on the spot in public**

- ❋ Claiming you "owe" it to them or others

- ❋ "It's expected"

- ❋ "It's a tradition"

- ❋ The promise of publicity, fame, fortune, respect, or some other wildly enriching, exciting, exclusive, highly profitable opportunity or reward

Let go of the need to know all, control all.

You can't be everything and do everything for everyone. Furthermore, it's not up to you to control and monitor every detail of everyone else's world or solve everyone's issues and challenges. Take a few steps back, be okay with a little uncertainty, and know there will always be challenges in others' lives. Joyously fire yourself as Self-Appointed General Manager of the Universe. It may feel odd at first, but as you get used to it, it will feel terrific.

There will be times when you absolutely, positively can't say no to a request or a situation. For example, you may be asked to help out a friend or family member who is facing a genuine crisis. You may have to miss a critical client meeting to care for your sick child or take on an assignment or role that will help you earn enough money to get through a serious financial crisis. Sometimes you just have to do what you have to do.

In many situations, however, you may realize that you have more choice in the matter than you think. Stop for a moment, carefully, mindfully review what's important to you, what your most highly valued standards and goals are, and (this is key) what alternatives or options are possible. Measure the alternatives against what someone is asking of you or what you are tempted to do. You'll see just how often your answer can still be no or even "not now."

Perhaps you are in a place where someone has done a tremendous favor for you and they've asked you to reciprocate. Tread carefully here. First, never do anything in return that is not in line with your morals or true capabilities. Second, if you cannot do what the other person is asking of you, say so but offer something else or offer to help at another time. You can't always be the recipient of help from others without somehow responding in kind.

The more you think about what you want and the more you practice assertively and confidently saying no to what you don't want, the stronger and more mindful, precise, and diplomatic your decision-making skills will get. You will free up time, energy, and resources to say yes to what you do want. You cannot make progress without practice.

Organizational expert and author Lorie Marrero reminds us that we actually teach others how to treat us. What's more, we often set ourselves up for situations that create more demands, work, and interruptions. She says, "Think about what you are putting out there. For example, if you don't like people to call you on your cell phone, don't give out that number. If you don't like to receive lots of emails, restrain yourself on how many you send out."

* * *

Delete the words "should" and "have to" from your vocabulary. Those are word choices that we often put upon ourselves when really we do have choices and options. Try mindfully using words such as "want to" and "choose to" instead.

* * *

handling requests and other distractions

Serve others, but keep it in perspective. Giving of yourself, doing favors, and being of service to others are part of what make you a good person and business person. It is important to remember the universal benefits of doing good deeds: generating good karma, paying it forward, helping out those who have helped you, and enjoying the glow of helping out the person who can never pay you back.

However, if you're not clear on your own needs, purpose, and goals, when your tendency is to always give too much, when you have people in your life who are chronic takers, and when you have a chronic need to give in order to feel needed, that's when it's easy to morph from champion to helper to martyr to doormat. At that point, you are cheating yourself out of the precious time, energy, resources, and focus to accomplish what is truly yours to do.

There's a popular saying that suggests you put your own oxygen mask on before helping someone else put on theirs. Another favorite saying states that you can't possibly fill another's warehouse if yours is empty. Both are true and worth remembering.

> Just because someone asks, it doesn't mean you are obligated to always say yes. Requests are the *beginning* of a negotiation. In the end, it should be a win-win. Before you tender a decision that helps someone out, think about how you can make the situation work for you as well.

Many requests made by others are impulsive. Try delaying your response to the person asking. You may discover that their need goes away or is fulfilled by someone else.

Even if someone gets cold, angry, or frustrated with you for saying no, they will eventually get over it or find another solution. And if they don't, what does that tell you about their respect for you and your time?

Some people can be gracious, humble, and focused in their requests, which makes it easy, quick, and delightful to respond to them and help them out. In contrast, some people can be downright rude, audacious, demanding, and draining. Be prepared for these vastly different personalities and requests and for how you will identify and respond to them.

Be aware that some requests might actually be great opportunities. Some requests can be timely and provide valuable experiences and opportunities. Consider such requests carefully. Perhaps even adopt a new policy: don't respond right away. Ask for at least a day or two to think about them. Compare your intended response to your purpose, vision, and goals. Then decide. Such requests can include:

- **Making or receiving an introduction or referral.**
- **Attending a meeting as someone's guest.**
- **Accepting an invitation to a lunch or coffee.**
- **Speaking, being a panelist, or emceeing an event.**
- **Reviewing or previewing a book.**
- **Reading and critiquing a resume or website.**
- **Offering a testimonial quote or providing a reference.**
- **Writing an article.**
- **Judging a competition.**

Often these are excellent opportunities. But they can also be a waste of time or devalue your expertise and business. Consider what exactly the opportunity is, who and what is involved, how much time investment is required, who the audience is, why they chose you, and so on.

If it sounds like a good fit and a commitment you can take on without taking too much time from your other activities and goals, go for it. If not, decline gracefully or suggest someone else they could ask.

Communications professional Lynn "Lindy" Segall offers this tip: when someone is making a request of you, ask for specifics on what they are doing and what *exactly* they need from you (time, expertise, money, leadership). This quick survey helps them get clear on their needs and helps you determine if it's a good fit for you. Additionally, you may be able to offer an alternative to their request that is easier for you to fulfill and still gives them the results they're seeking. For example, if they need your expertise, you may be able to have one meeting with them to download the information they need. They are happy, and you've fulfilled a request efficiently. Segall adds, "Finally, don't get swept up into their dream at the expense of your own."

Oh, those darn interruptions!

If you're like me, you may have a social or spontaneous streak that enjoys people, good conversation, relationship building, and refreshing breaks from the daily grind. These can be energizing gifts, but they can also be annoying, productivity killers and chronic energy depleters. These interruptions can include people who call you or drop by your office unannounced to do one or more of the interactions in the lists that follow. Note that one list has a positive connotation while the other is less so. Be aware of which you will accept as a positive, energizing break and which you will avoid like the plague.

Types of interruptions: what others do to energize or deplete you

Positive/Energizing	Negative/Depleting
Socialize	Talk endlessly
Share news	Engage in malicious gossip
Share information	Pump you for information
Discuss pertinent news	Rehash what's in the tabloids
Celebrate a victory	Brag
Offer sincere congratulations	Offer cynical or jealous comments
Get an objective opinion	Bug you for free advice
Discuss possible solutions	Whine, vent, or complain
Take a little work break	Hide from their responsibilities
Offer you a delicious treat	Mooch
Offer gratitude	Ask for another favor

It's up to you to educate and be firm, clear, and consistent with others about your policies, either proactively or as requests come up. The more clearly others know and understand your policies, limits, and boundaries – and how serious you are about preserving them – the less likely they will be to approach you without first thinking it through. They will no longer see you as an easy target.

working from home has unique challenges

Interruptions rise to a whole new level when you have a home office.

Family members may assume that just because you're not in a traditional office setting (and often within arms' reach) anything goes and you are at their beck and call.

I remember the time our son wandered through my office bouncing a basketball while I was on the phone with an important client! Fortunately, my important client worked from home as well and was understanding. Still, I had to educate our son on House Rules, including the right way to interrupt me if he needed me, and when extraneous noise wasn't appropriate or helpful.

My friend Angela remembers when she left her nine-to-five job to start her own real estate business out of her home. Family, friends, and neighbors knew she was working for herself and setting her own hours. Before the ink was dry on Angela's business cards, they began to ask more favors of her. "Can you take grandma to the doctor next week?" "Can you take Johnny his lunch at school? He forgot it again." "Can you feed and walk my dog while I'm on vacation?" "Can you drive me to the airport?" "Can you watch for a delivery for me?" "Can you wait at my home for the repair technician?"

"I really like to help other people out, but it just got out of control – and I let it. For some reason, everyone thought that because I didn't work at a conventional job, I had all the free time in the world," says Angela. "They saw me at home more, knew I was my own boss and set my own hours, but they never saw the lights on in my home office at midnight or realized that when they were enjoying their weekend I was often still working. They just assumed I was available and able to take on all their requests. My family members became the worst culprits. They threw everything in my lap. I had to educate them about what it was like to have my own business and what the challenges and realities were, learn to say no, and say it regularly, firmly, and without guilt."

Janet had a similar story only it pertained to her new practice as a career consultant. "I have a lot of friends and colleagues and I love networking and meeting people," she says. "It's been great for my business on a lot of levels, except for one – some people think I'm available 24/7 to provide free advice, answer their questions, watch for potential clients or job opportunities for them, speak at their meetings, or serve on their committees. All without any compensation. They totally forget that many of these requests are how I make my living. And worst of all, I've let them take advantage of me, all in the name of 'exposure' and demonstrating what I can do. One of my friends advised me to stop auditioning for the part!"

try this!

Employ a timer and a private setting to stay on task.

Amy McGeady, a proposal development consultant, frequently uses timers to budget her time for meetings as well as projects. "When I know the clock is ticking, I'm better at staying focused and completing tasks without interruptions or self-delay tactics." She also will frequently work at the local library when she has to focus without interruptions. She likes having a setting where there is no coffee being served, no music, few distractions, and little chance of running into a chatty friend or colleague.

Schedule and honor appointments with yourself. That's time-tested advice from Nishi Whitely, a business consultant and owner of Turn-lane Consulting, a practice that helps entrepreneurs at the crossroads of their businesses. Nishi reminds her clients that their time is their "life force" – an asset to be protected and used wisely. She also encourages them to schedule sixty- to ninety-minute appointments with themselves at least once or twice a day to work on top-priority projects. "Block these off on your schedule as appointments. No one needs to know this is an appointment with you. Honor these as you would other appointments and obligations. This single tip alone can help make it easier for business owners to make the shift from working *in* their businesses to working *on* their businesses."

the brain-picker dilemma

Jolene recalls the day she received an audacious and unexpected phone call from a friend of a friend who wanted to launch a business that would be in direct competition to hers in the same business community. The person was seeking not only free advice on how to set up her business, but also copies of Jolene's business and marketing plans, legal documents, and other highly proprietary materials.

"I could not believe what I was hearing," says Jolene. "After I got over the initial shock, I asked this person to explain to me why she thought I should be inclined to do this for her. She was silent and after a few moments realized how out of line her request was."

When you have talents, skills, experience, connections, influence, or other resources that people value, it can make you very attractive. This is great! However, you may also be more vulnerable to the scourge of endless requests for free advice and brain-picking.

Sure, it can feel flattering and even fulfilling to be a trusted confidante, advisor, problem-solver, mentor, and brainstorm partner; the person who everyone turns to for wise counsel. But it can wreak havoc with your concentration, schedule, energy levels, business, profitability, and even your reputation. This is particularly true if you make your living consulting and advising others. Doctors, lawyers, and other professionals are taught in their schooling how to avoid giving away their time and expertise. You can learn this too.

Learn to tell the difference between legitimate requests for advice and brain-picking. Here are two lists that show this difference.

Requests for advice	Brain-picking
Originates from a friend, colleague, or client	Originates from an acquaintance or stranger
Is a simple request (one or two questions)	Often involves elaborate problem-solving
Involves ten minutes or less	Involves more than ten minutes
A simple, humble, courteous request	A thoughtless, brazen, assuming request
Requester honors your value	Requester does not honor your value
Well-thought out, clear	Impulsive, fuzzy
Homework done, possible ideas prepared	No homework or ideas brought to the table
Framed with an offer to pay	Assumes it's free - now and always
Ready, able, and willing to reciprocate	No thought given to reciprocation; broken promises
Occasional, respectful	Frequent, repetitive, needy
Valued, effective, impactful	Often disputed or ignored
Requester is willing to do the work	Requester is seeking magic bullet
Requester is appreciative	Request is often demanding
One-time request	Repeated requests (with little action taken)

It's a good idea to create guidelines, policies, and requirements that will help ward off or manage potential Brain-Pickers. If you find that offering a certain amount of free advice actually works to help you attract business, develop relationships, try out new techniques, or gain valuable information or experience, go for it. Just be sure to create and stick to policies that make it clear what, when, and how much you are willing to share for free and when it's time to either end the conversation or transition into a paying relationship.

Samples of these guidelines, policies, and requirements might include:

❄ **Who you are willing to assist.**

❄ **Time limits per session.**

❄ **How many sessions you can fit into your schedule per week or month.**

❄ **How many questions the person can ask.**

❄ **What types of questions you can (and cannot) address.**

❄ **When you are available for these free sessions.**

❄ **How the person must contact you (e.g., by email, by phone, at your office).**

❄ **What they must prepare in advance.**

❄ **What else you might be doing during your time together (e.g., exercising, walking, or driving somewhere).**

❄ **How long they may have to wait for your response if it's a written request.**

❄ **What they must do as a prerequisite or as a follow-up (e.g., volunteer for a certain organization you support, mow your lawn, help you in some other way).**

❈ A "let's get clear" policies conversation so you know exactly what expectations are.

❈ A written "let's get clear" policies document you can share with the person making the request.

Here are some additional phrases you can use to test the waters when someone asks for your advice. They assert your boundaries and policies, but also open the door for attracting a potential client or valuable associate.

"That's exactly the kind of work I do with my clients. Would you like information on my schedule and fees?"

"I don't have time to talk about this right now, but I'd be delighted to have you contact me (or my assistant) so you have information on my schedule and fees. I'm guessing it may take several sessions to cover that topic adequately."

"I'd be open to a conversation on how we'd work together on this."

"That sounds like an interesting dilemma. Call me next week to schedule an appointment. My fee schedule is posted on my website."

"I'm so sorry. I have a very full schedule for the next few months and just don't have the time or resources to advise you on this right now."

"I'm sorry, I have to stay focused on serving my clients right now. If you'd like to learn more about how to become a client, please let me know."

> Be clear and asserting, but also gracious. Remember that you always have the right and the power to say "no thank you" to any request that does not work for you or takes you away from your priorities. You also don't want to alienate or repel someone who could become a paying client or a valuable referral source.

Ask what the person has already learned and/or tried. If you are the first person they've approached, suggest that they do some research on the topic first. The person can then share with you a list of possible solutions they are considering. This homework assignment often weeds out people who aren't serious about at least trying to solve their own challenges.

Educate others about your free advice policies.

To prevent a stream of brain-pickers sent by your well-meaning colleagues, be upfront and clear with others about your policies. For example, if you receive an email from someone requesting free advice and they mention your friend Steve recommended you, copy Steve on the email reply, which graciously states your policy on why you simply cannot honor the request (or under what conditions you can honor it). Steve will get the message.

Defer to other resources that might be helpful.

If you cannot help the person, offer another solution. This might include a referral to another expert who may have the time and be willing to offer free advice, or to another resource where the person can gather the information. Be cautious as you do this. Don't put the monkey on the back of someone who will not appreciate it. This will backfire on you.

Another option is to create a Frequently Asked Questions document that covers basic solutions for frequent requests. Or build a resource list of books, websites, and even public workshops, and webinars that might be helpful to people who want to build their knowledge in your areas of expertise. Offer this list in lieu of free one-on-one advising. You can also encourage them to visit your website, download any tips sheets or materials you offer there, or have them subscribe to your blog, if you have one.

Some consultants are willing to offer a low-cost entry-level service, such as a one-time free or discounted session. This can work or flop depending on how you utilize and structure it. Other ideas include offering occasional group sessions, workshops, and webinars at an affordable cost. It's also worth it to create helpful products that can appease the budget-conscious groupie as well as generate income for you, such as books, e-books, CDs, and other products.

Not all brain-pickers are cheap freeloaders. Some of them might be colleagues-in-training, or talented newbies who you would like to mentor. This can be a valuable relationship for the future. To make sure your mentoring relationships nurture you as well as your mentees, here are some suggestions. First, define exactly what mentoring means to you. Mentor only one person at a time (or set your own number), or start a mentoring group you meet with once a month or quarter. Have potential mentees apply, and select the ones you feel are best suited to you. Establish a set mentoring time period, perhaps including a thirty-day trial. Lastly, let the mentee(s) know what you require of them – for example, they must follow your advice, they cannot miss a mentoring session, and they must give back in some way, perhaps by mentoring someone else.

What if you're the one asking for a favor or free advice? Here are my suggestions on how to handle being on the other side of this fence:

- **Above all, show respect for the person's time, position, and expertise.**

- **Do your homework regarding your dilemma and possible solutions.**

- **Be very clear on the one or two things you want to ask this person.**

- **Be clear on why you selected the person in the first place.**

- ❈ Make no assumptions.

- ❈ Be considerate, gracious, and humble.

- ❈ Make it interesting, enticing, energizing, and fun to work with you.

- ❈ Return the favor. Make it a win for both of you.

- ❈ Don't expect that you will learn everything you need to know.

- ❈ Ask for no more than ten minutes.

- ❈ If you meet in person, show respect by being on time, prepared, and by dressing professionally.

- ❈ Send a sincere thank you, such as a written note or flowers.

- ❈ Never forget the value they've given you.

other focus- and productivity-killers

Beware of unwanted phone calls.

Virtual assistants, interns, answering services, voice mail, and caller ID are among the best inventions of all time. These allow you to screen your calls, ignore the phone, and receive messages you can deal with later (or not). How liberating is that?

Steve Haynes, owner of Fidelio Dogworks dog training service says his assistant is the key to preserving his schedule and upholding professional boundaries with clients. "I literally couldn't do what I do without her. She blocks calls, weeds out undesirable clients, manages my time, and is the gatekeeper between me and anyone who wants to talk to me all day long about their dogs without paying for the time."

Yet sometimes you may succumb to the allure of answering the phone, even while trying to focus on a more important task. If you must pick up – and there are certainly merits to being available – make it clear to the caller that you have only a few minutes to talk. Set a timer with an audible alarm if necessary.

Make and follow policies about emails and e-publications.

It's easy to say no to blatant spam. But what about all the e-newsletters, announcements, invitations, promotions, and other junk emails and email solicitations you receive? Delete and unsubscribe to anything you didn't specifically ask for or no longer want or find valuable. Be gracious in turning these down if you have relationships with the sender. Likewise, when you receive business cards from others, don't assume it automatically gives you permission to subscribe them to your e-lists. Any initial contact should be to seek permission to subscribe.

> The big debate: Is it really necessary to return or respond to every call, every voice message, and every email? Here are two points of view:
>
> *Yes.* Some people believe it is common courtesy and good customer service to reply to all phone calls and emails.
>
> *No.* Since many are pure solicitations, obnoxious or unwelcome requests, and time wasters, essentially "junk" you didn't ask for, it's acceptable to treat them as such and delete them without responding.

Manage your social media: Facebook, LinkedIn, Plaxo, Twitter, and others.

These can be valuable relationship-building, promotional, and information-gathering tools – and they can also be tremendous time-wasters. Be mindful in how you use them, if you choose to use them at all. Here are a few tips that may help you manage and leverage your social media interactions:

- ❄ **Develop, implement, and regularly review policies for when, how, how often, and why you will use social media tools.**

- ❄ **Remember every post is a reflection on you and your brand.**

- ❄ **Don't get caught up in the number of contacts you have. Focus more on the quality of the relationships and caliber of the people.**

- ❄ **You don't have to say yes to every friend request or respond to every message.**

- ❄ **Block or unfollow anyone who is not adding value to your work or world.**

events, meetings, and one-on-ones

It can be appealing and gratifying to be invited to coffee, lunch, happy hour, dinner, parties, or other events by people, whether you've just met them or have known them for years. Problem is, you could spend most of your waking hours engaging with others this way, especially if you network a lot or have a large database of friends, colleagues, and clients. It would be fun, but it's not practical. Therefore it's vital for your own productivity and balance to set limits and guidelines that can help you pick and choose which invitations and get-togethers are priorities for you.

Ask yourself right now: how many invitations do you accept because you genuinely want to or because it's part of a strategy? In contrast, how many do you accept simply because you were invited or out of habit, proximity, curiosity, obligation, guilt, desperation, loneliness, boredom, or because everyone else was going? It's time to be more intentional in setting your schedule.

Scrutinize your policies about coffees/lunches/one-on-ones.

Recalling Ethan's story at the beginning of this chapter, it just wasn't possible or practical for him to have coffee or lunch with everyone on his list – or everyone who invited him. It's wonderful to be popular and in demand with a full lunch and coffee schedule, but it can also be stressful and throw you totally off-course as you try to follow your vision and intentions, get your daily work done, and achieve important goals. You also might find that people will approach you with an invitation to coffee, when what they are seeking is your advice, influence, or a sale.

It is liberating to take a hard look at these one-on-one appointments and create guidelines and policies to ensure these meetings are worth your time investment. Start by asking yourself some questions and develop a policy such as this one:

Anyone I agree to meet one-on-one over coffee or lunch must be:

- ❊ **An existing client or one of my top contacts.**

- ❊ **A potential talent candidate, client, or advocate.**

- ❊ **Someone with a clear goal, vision, or objective for getting together – more than simply a social visit.**

- ❊ **Trustworthy and of good reputation.**

- ❋ Referred to me by a well-regarded colleague who I know is particular.

- ❋ A "giver" seeking a win-win relationship.

- ❋ In a business or field that interests me or complements my business.

- ❋ Someone with whom I can exchange information and views – and learn.

- ❋ Likeable and energizing.

- ❋ Someone who shows up looking their best.

The most important point here is to begin making proactive decisions about which invitations really serve a purpose on your schedule. Here are some tips for managing one-on-one invitations:

Limit your one-on-ones to certain weeks, days, or times of day.

For example, you may set aside only two one-hour coffees and one two-hour lunch each week. When you've scheduled your quota for a given week, the next ones need to be scheduled farther out. Experiment with policies and scheduling that works for your needs and schedule. You are always free to make exceptions if absolutely necessary.

Limit these meetings to locations convenient to you.

Taking the time to drive to a mutually convenient location is a great idea, but can be time-consuming. Have locations in mind that are convenient to you or are easily merged with other errands or appointments.

Invite others to your office.

Let others know that your schedule only allows you to meet in person at your office. You not only avoid the drive time, you also have more control over how long the meeting lasts. When you need to conclude the meeting, simply stand up and say, "Thanks so much for coming by, [the person's name]. It's been a pleasure getting to know more about you." Being in your office also makes it clear that the meeting is a business appointment rather than a social call.

Set aside specific coffee-by-phone times.

If you are not able or willing to get together for a face-to-face meeting, try this technique offered by Jan B. King of eWomenPublishing Network, who advises saying: "My days are very full, so I'm afraid I can't go to coffee or lunch, but I could visit with you for thirty minutes early one morning by phone, say 7:30." If the person really wants to get to know you better, they will accept this arrangement and be willing to make it work. If not, it's their choice to decline.

Try the "How about now?" technique.

Let's say you just met someone at an event and they're interested in getting together to know you better. If your schedule allows (and you can be proactive in setting aside this time), suggest you meet for ten or fifteen minutes right after the event you are currently attending. Stay true to the time limit. After investing this relatively small amount of time with the person, you may be able to gauge whether or not a longer one-on-one date is in order down the road.

Let the person know about another group event you will be attending in the future.

If you are unable or unwilling to meet with someone one-on-one any time in the near future, let the person know what events you'll be attending next. If they want to converse with you again, they can choose to attend as well.

Request some additional information first.

You have every right to know as much as possible about anyone with whom you spend time. Ask for more information, such as a website, resume or CV, marketing materials, testimonials, or even the results of a survey or homework assignment you give them. For example, you could say, "You know, I'm just fascinated with people, but I really like to learn more about them before I meet with them one-on-one. So would you be so kind as to provide me with [state the type of information you want from them]." *Warning:* this sort of request might offend some people, particularly those who are overly sensitive, insecure, or have massive egos. But then you won't have to deal with them anymore, will you? Such a loss.

Limit the topics of discussion.

You're pretty sure that Person A wants to meet with you so she can vent (yet again) about her ex-husband, the job she hates, or her chronic health or financial problems. Or you've heard that Person B puts a long, aggressive sales pitch onto anyone he corners. With this intelligence, it's perfectly okay to create, communicate, and uphold some strict policies for what you will and will not discuss during one-on-ones. You might say, "I'd prefer to make this about getting to know each other, rather than a sales presentation." Or, "I'd be happy to meet with you, but let's keep the conversation strictly professional."

> Limiting what you will talk about often filters out those who have an agenda that's not agreeable to you. Remember, you are in control of whether you meet with these people or not. Make mindful choices. It's your precious time.

Set strict time limits and bring or state your preferred agenda.

Similar to the previous tip, you have every right to state how much time you can offer and how you'd like to spend that time. You might have a policy that states that first-time one-on-ones last thirty minutes, with each person allowed fifteen minutes to talk about their business and background. Bring written questions and pay attention to the time. The latter can be difficult, especially if you are enjoying yourself.

Say you're not available. Period.

This one can be both gracious and effective. "Thank you for the invitation, but I'm just not available to get together any time soon." Or, "Thanks for asking, but unfortunately my schedule just doesn't accommodate that type of get together right now." Who is to say or judge why you are not available, you just aren't. End of story.

You knew there'd be a however, didn't you? Here it is. However, remember these guidelines:

- ❈ **Be respectful and gracious.**
- ❈ **Don't burn bridges.**
- ❈ **Consider that relationships can be circumstantial, evolutionary, or cyclical.**
- ❈ **Don't forget the people who helped you get where you are today.**

professional memberships can be good and not-so-good

There is often merit in being an active member of professional or business development organizations, as long as they're the right ones for you. What's more, networking should be a regular and ongoing part of any business plan. However, is it possible that, purely out of habit, you are currently a member of an organization or attending networking events that aren't serving you? Give it some thought.

If an event, association, or group isn't energizing you, if you don't look forward to going to the gatherings, if the programs aren't enriching for you, and if you aren't getting what you need professionally or personally, ask yourself why. Perhaps it's no longer the right fit for you. Or you might consider your own attitude or how you are approaching and working the event. Or perhaps you can maintain your association, just not attend every meeting. Analyze the investment in time, energy, resources, and attention you're giving the membership. Would that investment be better used in another way? Commit to a solution or quit altogether. Or even just take a break from it. If you find yourself missing it, go back.

As with events and memberships, serving on committees, volunteering, and accepting leadership roles can either drain or sustain you. Have you ever been sucked into serving as a leader or committee member when you would rather not? Or maybe you agreed to say yes purely because no one else stepped up to the plate. Make sure that any time you agree to serve as a volunteer, committee member, chairperson, or officer of an organization that it offers some form of a "win" for you. It's honorable to serve and give back, but not at the expense of your business, health, family, or other priorities.

I calculated the investment I made in serving an organization several years ago and discovered that it was equivalent to more than $25,000 of my professional time. It was a fun responsibility and I received value beyond dollars for my role, including valuable connections, stronger relationships, publicity, and reputation building. But I also knew when it was time to step down, put that time and energy back into my own business and projects, and let someone else have the opportunity.

My colleague Joyce has a specific "Giving Back" plan. She tithes 10% of her working hours to an association or non-profit that she carefully selects each year. This plan keeps her involved, ensures she is giving back to her industry, helps her stay focused and disciplined on where and how she gives, and creates a definitive formula and boundaries for her. Whenever she is asked for more than she can give, she can graciously say no, feeling confident she has indeed made a significant contribution. No guilt allowed. Joyce changes which group she assists each year, which allows her to spread her "wealth" across many different types of people and causes.

Before you consider how you will give back, determine realistically how much of your time and resources you can give. When presented with a request or opportunity, decide if the role is truly one you are suited for – one that showcases your strengths, allows you to work with people you want to know better, teaches you the lessons you want to learn, or gives you the experience or connections you desire.

You can ask for documentation on what the obligation entails, such as a list of responsibilities. Take a look at your upcoming commitments – is it the right time to take on an additional responsibility?

If you do decide to take on this role, set limits up front, request that agendas and timekeepers be used at any meetings, build a team of helpers and delegate some tasks, and create systems to build in efficiency. If you decline the opportunity to serve, you might create a role that does work for you, or split the duties of another role, or offer to be an ad hoc advisor available by phone.

Susan, a freelance copywriter with a thriving business and a school-age daughter, agreed to serve on a committee for her daughter's school festival. The committee met once a week and was comprised mostly of stay-at-home moms. Susan enjoyed getting to know the other moms, being able to serve on the committee, and offering her ideas and talents. But she was frustrated that the meetings, which began at 8:00 a.m., dragged on for most of the morning. The other moms who didn't have jobs or businesses to run enjoyed this opportunity to gather, work on the festival plans, and socialize. Susan, however, had projects to work on, deadlines to meet, and other obligations.

Rather than create a huge fuss, Susan came up with a win-win solution. She let the others know that while she loved their company, she had one hour to spend on the meetings. She offered to be in charge of providing an agenda and keeping the meeting on track. Then if the others wanted to stay on, finish up any details, and keep visiting they could do so. All agreed that would work.

Susan reports that the following meetings ran far more efficiently, the committee members stayed on task, and everyone was happy, including Susan who could be on her way and resume her workday.

what do you do if you want to "fire" a client?

James had spent several years in a job he didn't like in an environment he found nothing short of toxic. He finally decided it was not healthy for him to spend more than forty hours a week in this situation and turned in his resignation. He went out on his own as an author's assistant, but was worried, as many new solopreneurs are, about whether he'd attract enough business to pay the bills. Coming from this place of fear, James took on a client he instinctively knew probably wasn't a good fit for him.

But, hey, a client is a client and he had money to spend. James quickly discovered that working with this unsavory fellow was just as bad, if not worse, than working in his previous job. "I had to get very brave, but I knew I had to do it, even though he was my biggest client," James says. "I resigned from this client and recommended he work with someone else." Within a few weeks several more pleasant and suitable clients appeared and filled the gap.

While many clients are the lifeblood of your company and are to be valued, served, and respected, some can make your life miserable, as was the case with James. Clients who aren't a fit for you or your business, who don't respect, appreciate, or value what you do for them, who make extreme demands and withhold payments, then whine for faster turnaround and better prices, are definitely not the kinds of clients worth keeping. They are the clients you just can't please no matter how hard you try. They eat up your time and resources, drive you crazy, and end up costing you money. Go ahead. Let them go. Refer them to your least favorite competitor. Trust me, you won't miss them.

In addition, many wise professionals have specific policies and practices about clients to avoid from the start. A friend who owned a successful PR firm had a strict "No Mean People" philosophy. Others embrace the practice of firing at least one client a year.

* * *

There are many good ways to say no and can be the difference between offering great customer service and being a doormat. The latter will not earn you profitability, happiness, or respect.

* * *

conscious business development

As a business person there are few things as exciting as the possibility of landing a new client. This means you may be tempted to go to any length to win the new business. But remember to be conscious of how much time you are willing to invest and risk on cultivating new business, and how much you are willing to give to prove yourself. Consider developing standards and policies on the amount of time and resources you can realistically invest on business development. How much information is worth sharing in proposals and meetings? What are you willing to give, knowing that you may not win the business?

Take regular breaks and retreats to revisit and reassess everything you are doing and the companies and people you are working with. I call these "reflection breaks." Sometimes these take just an hour or so of quiet time. Sometimes I go on a mini-retreat or arrange a mini-sabbatical, because things change, and so do we. This gives me the 35,000 foot view and allows me to review my mission, vision, intentions, and goals. I ask myself what's working and what's not, and ponder possible solutions to current challenges. I question everything – is this *really* right for me? Is it *still* right for me?

These breaks allow you to adjust, make changes, and create new policies accordingly. You will know the ground you stand on, and why you stand there. You will be able to hold steady and stay the course you have mapped out. All without falling prey to manipulation or guilt.

why do this work?

When you can become clear on what works for you and your business and what does not, when you can be more confident and firm on when it's appropriate to say no to whatever no longer serves you, benefits begin to multiply. Because you will have better clarity and focus, you'll have more time, energy, and resources for what matters to you in your business, in your relationships, and in your life. You will enjoy improved productivity and profitability, greater freedom and peace of mind, and reduced stress. Most importantly, others will accord you the respect you deserve.

✳ build connections

CULTIVATING YOUR MOST VALUABLE RELATIONSHIPS

In this chapter, you will:

- Learn how to recognize and maintain relationships with "your people."

- Find tips on how to connect and stay in touch.

- Discover how your impact on others impacts you.

- Understand that your attitude matters.

Judy had just launched her consulting business. She was excited about doing corporate work as well as hosting international workshops and seminars. She had cut her teeth doing projects with several household-name companies while employed with a larger training firm. Her training had placed her in a special niche that few people were serving. It seemed like the perfect time to venture out on her own.

She began attending professional and networking events each month, scattering herself across many different organizations and handing out lots of business cards and brochures. While on the networking circuit, Judy made contact with many people who understood the importance and unique qualities of her work and appreciated her special niche. These people seemed to be excited about letting others know about her work and possibly partnering with her or making some cross-referrals.

After her first important year in business, Judy pared back on her networking efforts. She chose not to join any of the organizations whose networking events she had attended. She rarely attended more than one meeting per group. She also turned down many offers to go to lunch or coffee, even with her most promising contacts. She thought she had already done a good job of getting the word out and believed it was time to set aside her connections efforts and focus on other aspects of her work, such as planning several workshops.

Judy's business never took off. At best, business flowed at a trickle. Then it dried up altogether. Judy was forced to cancel several of the workshops she had planned due to poor response. She couldn't understand what went wrong. She'd let people know who she was and she'd gotten the word out. Furthermore, she was sending out regular email announcements about her services and events. That should have kept her connections aware and interested in what she had to offer, right? Isn't it as simple as that?

Unfortunately, it's not.

connections require cultivation

What Judy didn't realize was that going on an aggressive but spotty networking tour followed up by email blasts and newsletters isn't enough to build a business and a database of solid contacts, clients, and supporters. You have to commit to putting regular effort into building *and maintaining* your most valuable connections and relationships, especially if you expect to earn and maintain visibility, trust, loyalty, business, and referrals. If you don't make this a regular habit, you won't be remembered or you'll drift into the background.

I can relate to what Judy experienced. I had a similar wake-up call several years ago. I had become very busy with one regular client and felt somewhat smug. I decided that all I wanted to do was focus on my work with them. I stopped attending events and didn't bother to reach out to my other clients, colleagues, and peers regularly.

When I finally ventured out one evening to a grand opening party hosted by one of my colleagues, I heard something that hit me like a two-by-four between the eyes. A former client came over to me and said, "Patti DeNucci! Great to see you! I heard you'd moved or retired."

What?

I was shocked. But after giving it some thought, I could see how my peers had come to that conclusion. I had disappeared off the net-working circuit and cocooned myself in my home office. It was a reminder that my best and most valuable relationships required care and feeding, even when I was busy. If I didn't tend to them, the relationships would wither and die.

discover "your people"

To quote consultant Alecia Huck of Maverick & Company, "Your people are your people." In other words, you probably know certain people with whom you feel the most comfortable, energized, and inspired. These are the people who bring a smile to your face when you pick up the phone and hear their voice. When you see them at an event, you rush over to greet them. Every encounter adds something valuable and special to your life or your work. They challenge you, encourage you, nurture, and support you. They are your people; members of your tribe.

Your people may give you good advice or send business referrals or opportunities your way. These are the people who may go out of their way to do a favor for you, show up when you invite them to an event, send you a warm thank you note, or cheer you up when you feel down. They may invest in you or your business in some way. Likewise, you have been eager and happy to give back to them similarly. The flow has been natural, reciprocal, and trusting. It's never necessary to keep score. And of course your people can also be your favorite clients.

Jim Cathcart, CSP, CPAE, award-winning speaker, and author of more than fifteen books including *Relationship Selling* and *The Acorn Principle*, offers a wise saying about connections and relationships. He says, "People who 'get it' are those who show you that they understand who you are, what you care about, and how you feel. They are also people who recognize the limits to what they know about you and they are still eager to learn more about you."

I see another dimension here as well. The people who "get it" understand what the world, life, and business are really about. It's not always about who is best at working a room, selling widgets, making money, and being smart or powerful. It goes much deeper than that.

It involves having a purpose, believing in timing and synchronicity, pursuing long-term, mutually beneficial relationships, living and working with integrity, and making a positive impact on the world.

* * *

*When you meet someone and you say to yourself,
"This person "gets it," what does that mean for you?
What does 'getting it" mean to you?*

* * *

You can apply the wisdom of who your people are to all kinds of relationships in your world – personal as well as professional. It can serve as a measuring stick or filter by which you determine if someone is a good fit for you or not. You may never look at any connection or relationship the same way ever again. Your perspective on people, connections, and relationships will be forever shifted.

Not everyone can be "your people." Accept that some people may not be a fit, initially or ever. You may meet or know people with whom you just don't sense or experience a high level of mutual commitment and connection. Nothing personal. They are just not a fit for you. That's okay. It's all about priorities.

Consider this, though: you may change your mind about some people as you learn more about them, see them in action, or hear what others have to say about them. With time or as circumstances change, you may feel differently about them and possibly even be inclined to make a connection.

For example, while at a conference I was introduced to a woman who several other colleagues felt I should absolutely, positively get to know as we have similar businesses, but in separate parts of the country. (Those are often great connections to have, by the way.) I'll call her Samantha. My first conversation with her was not what I'd expected. Samantha was reserved and seemed disinterested in our conversation. I almost sensed resentment; as if she had not wanted to meet me and wanted to end the conversation. I was not impressed with the connection at all.

Later that day I saw my colleague Jane conversing with Samantha. They were laughing and smiling. That evening I asked Jane what her impressions of Samantha were. I received a thumbs-up. "She's really lovely. You should try talking to her again," said Jane. So I did. In doing so, I learned that immediately before my first conversation with Samantha, she had received a phone call with bad news about her aunt. No wonder she had not seemed cordial or happy. Who would? Needless to say I'm glad I gave Samantha a second chance. Today we are fast friends.

try this!

Do you know of someone who you would like to connect with, but haven't yet? Follow these rules to reach out to them:

- Be sure you know why you want to add them to your circle.

- Take every step in the process with the utmost care, humility, and tact.

- Approach them with respect and courtesy. An email or letter is least intrusive.

- If you have a mutual contact, ask for an introduction.

- Explain why you want to meet as well as the value you wish to bring them.

- Let them know what you admire about them (without sounding like a star-struck fan).

- Make no assumptions on their interest in replying or responding in kind.

- Don't take a no or "not now" personally.

- Be patient. They may not be interested initially, but with time that could change.

- Allow for divine timing and synchronicity.

- Don't cross the line from professionally persistent to stalker!

make your people your top priority

Remember the 80:20 rule? Twenty percent of the people in your professional database are the ones who bring you the most results and value. Focus on them.

Stay in touch with your Top 20%. Call them on the phone. Meet with them in person when possible. Ask what you can do for them. Let them know what you're trying to do and what they may be able to do for you. Express your gratitude to them promptly and regularly for the many ways they create value for you.

> Among the best assets you can have in business are your connections and relationships with your best, most energizing and valuable clients, colleagues, and friends – your people. Invest in your connections with them. Keep them going and growing.

Pare back on random networking.

My friend Laurel, a seasoned and successful real estate agent, was among the first to inspire me to do this. One day over lunch she revealed that once she had built up a solid database of ideal clients, colleagues, friends, and connections, she decided to spend much less time on group networking activities. Instead of attending one or two larger events each week, she began investing some of this time in one-on-one meetings, nurturing the existing relationships that meant the most to her. Laurel also co-hosted smaller, more exclusive gatherings and scheduled regular coffees and lunches. These more intimate get-togethers allowed more time to have the longer, more meaningful conversations that allowed relationships to grow, deepen, and flourish. "I simply decided to play the hand I held, rather than try to add more to it," Laurel says. Wise advice.

> Growing and maintaining your best and highest quality
> relationships is one of the best things you can do for your
> business in the long run. It is generally far more powerful
> than occasional or random spurts of manic, marathon, or
> drive-by networking.

Be patient, diligent, and willing to invest the time it takes to get to know your people. Building quality relationships requires time, effort, finesse, sharing, reflection, and an equitable flow of energy. There are many additional ways to build these relationships with your people; the following suggestions are just a few.

Attend the events "your people" attend.

This means asking them about their favorite networking venues and groups, and then attending occasionally as well. If you know one of your key people is attending a particular event and you are also attending, ask if they'd like to schedule some time together before the meeting, during any networking phase of the meeting, or after the meeting. You may even decide to sit together during the meal or program. Be sure not to dominate all their time and be mindful that they will likely have other connections to make during the event.

Invite them to attend or be your guest at an event you believe they will like.

Whether it's a networking event, a luncheon where there's an intriguing speaker, a book signing with an author you know or admire, or whatever else you can think of, invite a favorite colleague or someone you want to get to know better to attend as your guest. And don't forget to introduce them to some of your friends and colleagues while you're there. They will remember this special VIP treatment.

Accept their invitations whenever possible.

If one of your people invites you to an event they are hosting or offers to bring you as a guest, do your best to accept, particularly if it sounds like a fit for you. Be sure to thank them and reciprocate!

Plan and invite your top contacts to strategic small gatherings.

A gathering of four to twenty of your most valuable colleagues over lunch, cocktails, or dinner can be a refreshing break from large events that can be noisy, crowded, and overwhelming. Plus you have more time to converse and connect. So why not host one? When creating your invitation list consider what those on your list will have in common and whether you've created a good blend. Plan the event and send out invitations well in advance. Remember to send out a reminder a few days prior. Also make it clear on whether there is any cost to attend. For example, is it a party you are throwing for your friends and hosting? Or is it a casual Dutch Treat gathering?

* * *

Connecting events you host should be free
of heavy sales pitches. This is about connecting,
not promoting or selling.

* * *

Volunteer or serve on a committee together.

Working shoulder to shoulder is a great way to get to know each other better, see each other in action, and help each other out, all while strengthening your bonds, learning new skills, and making a difference to others.

Do business with your people if it's a good fit.

By all means do business with the people you know, like, respect, and trust whenever possible. For example, if you can buy your shoes at a shop owned by a colleague, by all means do so. If you can host your next gathering at an establishment that donated a gift certificate to the fundraising committee you served on, that is great as well. Use the power of your purse to build connections and support your best colleagues whenever possible. Maintain professional boundaries when these transactions take place and never assume or expect you will receive discounts or freebies.

Share pertinent or useful information.

Point out news on important events in your industry, or blogs, videos or newsletters you think your people might enjoy. If you saw one of your people mentioned in the media, it's a good idea to send them a clip or link to let them know you saw it, and congratulate them. I love it when a thoughtful colleague shares an article, quote, interesting fact, link, or other resource with me that is exactly in line with something I care about, was searching for, or am working on. I even enjoy the occasional funny story, joke, or cute greeting. The more closely it matches my tastes and interests the better. It doesn't have to cost a thing except a few minutes – and a keen understanding of what is appropriate and appreciated.

A word of caution here – there is an art to this type of connecting. It's not so much email blasting as it is a very personal, highly customized sharing of information. Anything you send should indicate your level of interest in and understanding of who the person is, how busy they are, what they value, and what they are working on. Ask yourself whether their reaction will be a delighted "Ah!" or an irritated "Ugh! Not another one!" (followed closely by a swift click of the Delete button). In short, when in doubt, don't send it out. Resist emailing or posting:

- ❋ **Email blasts to all your contacts for random items that catch your attention.**

- ❋ **Chain mail or emails that require you to "send this email to ten people in the next ten minutes."**

- ❋ **Inappropriate jokes.**

- ❋ **Too-good-to-be-true offers or contests.**

- ❋ **Any newsflash or consumer warning that you've not checked out on Snopes.com or otherwise determined is not a hoax, scam, or spam.**

- ❋ **Links or attachments that could result in spam or viruses.**

more ideas for making staying in touch part of your routine

More ways you can add value to relationships with your people or Twenty Percenters include nominating them for awards, honoring them with an award of your own, writing a testimonial for them, planning a gathering in their honor, presenting them with a token gift, coupon, or gift certificate they might enjoy, or swapping ideas, advice, or feedback.

> Success does not happen in a bubble. Your most valuable business relationships are the keys to maximizing your success in business, whether you are a solopreneur or an employee of a large company.

Think long term and make staying in touch a regular habit. Like anything good that grows, rewarding relationships require care, feeding, and time. No matter how busy you get or how successful and secure you may feel, tending to your most valued relationships should be a regular, sustainable habit. It should be an activity you intentionally engage in all year, not randomly, seasonally, or when you desperately need more business or a big favor. And just to be clear, sending out a sales promotion once a quarter does not equate to being in touch. This is not how to build relationships with your people.

For example, two acquaintances I see often at local business events send me regular, sales-pitchy emails that I never asked for and would prefer not to receive. After several attempts to release myself from their email lists, I've diverted the unwanted promotions to my spam file. These contacts may believe they are "staying in touch" with me or "have a relationship" with me, but what they are really doing is filling my inbox with junk I never asked for and do not appreciate. As a result, they are pushing me farther and farther away with each wave of spam. Don't do this to others.

Decide on a benchmark standard for how and how often you want to be in touch with your best contacts. You might decide that once a month or once a quarter is ideal. Or you may decide that you'll reach out to two or three key contacts in some friendly, non-sales-pitchy form each day or several each week. Different connections may require different schedules. Setting up some kind of plan and database with note-keeping features will help you track how often you're in touch with various people.

Varying your methods of reaching out is also a good idea. Electronic and social media methods are fast and efficient ways to stay in touch. Regular email messages have their place. But in this day and age it's a special surprise to receive a thoughtful hand-written note or a "just thinking of you" phone call now and then. And of course nothing can replace getting together face-to-face. Vary and balance how you stay in touch with others and note which methods work best for each person. Using different techniques keeps it interesting and fresh. Make notes on what methods your people prefer.

Haven't heard from Mary in months? Bob seems to have fallen off the face of the earth? It's okay. If you value these contacts and if you've had a great relationship with them in the past, give them the benefit of the doubt. Take the initiative and reach out to them if it's been awhile. People who are driven, successful, innovative, and energizing may be in the throes of a big project, traveling, ill, focusing on their families or personal matters, or even taking a well-deserved sabbatical. Give them a break. In fact, do more than that. Give them a call or send them an email or handwritten note. Make sure it's not a guilt-inducing message crying, "Why haven't I heard from you?" or "Where have you been?" Make it friendly, fun, and supportive.

Let them know you are thinking of them and hope all is well. They may be so incredibly focused (or distracted) that a refreshing piece of cheery correspondence could be just what they need.

* * *

Be the one who actually follows up and takes the next cordial step. So few people do.

* * *

If you've not tried it yet or are still just dipping your toe in the social media waters, learn how to strategically leverage the power of social media to stay connected and top of mind. Facebook, Twitter, and other social media and networking methods can be addicting and supreme time wasters, but they can also be invaluable, efficient tools that help you stay connected with very minimal effort. If you can create both a strategy and some limits on how to leverage this technology, it can help you stay in touch with your treasured friends, family, and contacts.

Remember to keep certain types of correspondence totally free of any business reference. Let's say you're sending someone a note of thanks or another greeting such as a birthday card or a message of congratulations. In cases like these, leave out any promotional messages. Think of how refreshing it is to receive a greeting free of any marketing message; one that focuses on celebrating and appreciating just you, the great person you are, or something noteworthy that you did.

tips for meeting and connecting in person

Have a date set to meet a colleague in person? Try setting a few intentions, preparing some questions, or even setting a basic agenda. While some of my best conversations with colleagues occurred totally on the fly and are social in nature, it's also important to have an idea of why you are getting together. It might be just to catch up on happenings in your respective worlds, but you may also have more to cover. You don't have to prepare or stick to a rigid agenda; that would take all the fun out of the meeting. Make a few notes on what you definitely want to talk about in your meeting, or what questions to ask. Being a natural, sincere, in-the-moment conversationalist is an important part of connecting. But being purposeful will help ensure that your time together isn't just more talking, but time well spent. This is particularly important when time is precious and you don't see the person very often.

Keep the conversation easy and natural. Don't make it sound or feel like an interview. Be respectful of privacy and boundaries. Pay attention to what the other person feels comfortable talking about.

> A note on professional courtesy: if you invite someone to lunch or coffee, particularly if you have a favor to ask them, it's up to you to pay the tab.

Know someone who is on a similar path to yours? Consider becoming accountability partners. See if they are willing to commit to checking in with you for thirty minutes by phone once a week. Here you can set and compare to-dos, measure progress, and encourage each other to stay the course. Or if you have a colleague who offers a service you need and you offer an area of expertise that you know they can use, schedule a swap session where you exchange services, connections, expertise, or information of equal value on the spot.

There's nothing like time in the car and a long stretch of highway to create or reinforce a bond. One way to do this is to take a road trip or attend a retreat or conference together. I had one of the most beneficial conversations of my entire career in a car driving to a conference with two colleagues who at the time I knew only casually. Today they are two of my most valued friends and advisors. I owe it all to that road trip. Four hours in the car each way gave us plenty of time to talk about our businesses and lives and to share what we were working on, what was working, what wasn't, and what our intentions were for the conference. It also gave us a chance to brainstorm about how we could help each other. It was nothing short of profound. The conference was pretty good, too, and furthered our blooming relationship.

Likewise, attending retreats can forge stronger relationships as it helps us get away from distractions and spend focused time together working on our lives and businesses.

try this!

Try the spontaneous, "come as you are" technique. This one won't work for everyone in your database, but with the right people, it can provide just the break and time together that you both need, particularly when it involves people you know fairly well. Simply pick up the phone and call them, inviting them to join you that day at a mutually convenient location, just as they are, for a one-hour, impromptu visit over coffee or tea. A favorite friend and colleague did this one day last fall, inviting several of us and admitting freely that she was wearing no makeup and was in her running attire. Three of us showed up, and we are still talking about what a delightful visit we had. In fact that visit spawned the idea for a weekend retreat together a few weeks later. I focused more time on this book now as a result of that time away together and the encouragement that I received. Lesson: sometimes spontaneity can create fantastic results!

worth remembering: basic human needs are to belong and feel valued

Military generals, athletic coaches, and business leaders all know this truth: when members of the team *like, value,* and *respect* each other, they build strong bonds. As a result, they will walk through fire for each other and achieve far greater results. With this in mind, the way to build strong bonds with your most valued clients, contacts, colleagues and friends, the "teammates" who will strengthen you and help you succeed, is to always take the time to greet them warmly and make connections with them as fellow humans before talking business.

To build and grow quality relationships, you must connect, establish a rapport, and reconnect on a human level first. Remember that you are, above all, people and people matter. They, like you, deserve courtesy and respect. Here are some tips about connecting and making others feel special.

Be authentic, open, human, and imperfect.

It's hard to make conversation, connect, or build a relationship with someone who is constantly in business or sales mode or isolates themselves with a hardened, impenetrable shell of perfection. In fact, it's possible to be credible and professional in addition to being authentic, open, and human. You don't have to unload all your dirty laundry, sad stories, secrets, or quirky traits, but it's okay to share a few notes from your personal life and be honest and real and even a little vulnerable when you meet and get to know others.

Be respectful of time and boundaries.

One way to make sure *no one* will want to get to know you or be your friend or colleague is to make sure you are full of yourself, pushy, needy, negative, intrusive, impatient, passive-aggressive, desperate, and drama-driven.

Years ago I actually had to stage a break-up with a needy, insecure colleague who would not leave me alone and wanted desperately, from the moment we met at a business function, to be my best friend and confidante. The relationship started out well enough, but after a few weeks I realized that her frequent calls and emails were always peppered with one needy request and drama after another. It was too much and the relationship veered from a professional alliance to one full of toxicity.

I tried dropping hints about how busy I was and that I needed to back away from the relationship for awhile. That didn't work. I moved to having a very clear and frank conversation with the woman about how she was crossing professional lines in our relationship. Still, her frantic, needy calls and emails continued.

Finally, I had to block the woman's phone number and divert her emails to my spam file. I still can't believe I had to take that step.

Be particular, but never a snob.

It's impossible to be everything to everybody, not everyone you meet will be a fit in your world, and you will probably even outgrow certain relationships. That said, it's still important to treat others with respect and graciousness.

> Employ courtesy and good manners. Polish up any of your rough edges, inside and out. Show up at your best ready to do business. Make every interaction patient, kind, warm, respectful, and positively memorable.

Be interested, not just interesting.

Some people may talk more than they listen in their relationships. Don't be that person. Listen more than you speak while holding up your end of the conversation. And give others your full interest and attention when conversing. Challenge yourself to learn and remember interesting or special facts about your people. They will remember you for it.

As you continue to define and refine the standards by which you measure the value of your relationships and "your people," don't forget to continually review and raise the standards of your own behavior. Make each day an opportunity to grow as a person and learn, develop, and raise the bar as a professional. Make choices each day that set you apart in the best possible ways.

keep the flow of energy going by giving first

When you are aware of who your people are and how they can be of value to you, it's equally important to know and be interested in what you can do for them. Be the first to give, keep the "energy exchange" flowing, and strive to be a valuable ally. There are many creative and easy ways to show support for your people.

My friend and colleague Leslie Roan is a great example of someone who gives first. She is a makeup artist and consultant for a large cosmetics company and has a strong background in corporate sales. She is one of the most professional, gracious, friendly, positive, and generous people I know. She is not your typical sales person nor does she treat her customers as participants in the achievement of her latest sales quota goals. Her customers are (or quickly become) valued colleagues and friends.

In addition to her long roster of clients, Leslie is well-connected in business and philanthropic circles and regularly hosts gatherings in her beautiful home. Every event I've attended that is hosted by Leslie is an A-ticket, not-to-be-missed event.

Leslie attracts her clients by giving them complimentary makeovers, particularly when they have a special event to attend, are having a photograph taken, or are going to be on television for an interview. This is at least a $150 value in time and expertise. When she does makeovers for her friends and customers, she gives them her full and undivided attention for at least an hour, complete with a perfect cup of coffee or tea served in a china cup and saucer. She will even touch up their hair. Thoughtful conversation happens in these sessions as well.

I walk out of Leslie's studio looking and feeling like a million bucks and ready to conquer the world. Sometimes I purchase her products and sometimes I don't. She doesn't keep track. But I'm far more likely to buy from her than from anyone else because I admire and respect how she treats others and does business.

Leslie is a shining example of someone who is successful as well as a giving, caring person. Why would I go to a stranger at a department store makeup counter when I can spend my time and money with her? And why would I not want all my friends and colleagues to know her?

Leslie's giving and gracious nature is a great reminder that it's not always about money. Often some of the most valuable business relationships involve no exchange of money whatsoever. They are the relationships that bring us support, advice, encouragement, ideas, industry news, and many other forms of valuable "capital." These can be just as valuable as the ones that fill our bank accounts. Sometimes even more so.

You may be surprised at how many relationships bring you value, even if there is no black-and-white (or green) way to measure it.

* * *

Forms of non-monetary value can include the following: advice, appreciation, ideas, inspiration, industry news, speaking opportunities, publicity, best practice information, expertise, introductions, recommendations, respect, credibility, referrals, connections, endorsements, encouragement, feedback, and just someone to listen to you. And more.

know how you impact others

How we affect others' moods and energy levels can make or break our relationships and connection with others. Reflect for a moment – do you believe you lift others up? Or bring them down? Or are you just another name in their database? Or among the people who are their Top Twenty Percenters? Are you always looking out for yourself? Or are you genuinely interested in others? Do you do all the talking? Or do you listen attentively as well?

Three colleagues recently told me why they were grateful for their relationships with me. They graciously noted that it's because I regularly inspire them, energize them, and add value to their work and their lives. They added that I seem to know just when to call or get in touch. Can you think of any greater compliments?

Being a valued colleague or contact isn't about offering a non-stop stream of compliments, being a "pleaser," or sucking up. It's about being someone who shares ideas and advice, engages in meaningful and timely conversations, listens with understanding, offers supportive comments, shows up with a positive attitude, expresses gratitude, and is a true and loyal peer. It's being a virtual teammate with their own vision and journey but who shares similar beliefs and passions.

Author of *The Ripple Effect* and networking expert Steve Harper calls this making "positive ripples." What kind of ripples are you creating in your business relationships? Positive, negative, or none at all?

According to a study in *The British Medical Journal* authored by Nicholas Christakis, Ph.D., a physician and professor of medical sociology at Harvard Medical School, happiness actually spreads beyond a single personal interaction. It can "ripple" as far as three connections away.

I believe this not only impacts others, but can affect your reputation as well.

> Take care to genuinely reflect your brand and diligently protect your reputation. Whether it's making a good first impression, staying true to your word, associating with people of the highest integrity, making quality referrals, or simply striving to do the right thing, a stellar reputation is priceless. Furthermore, if you're going to be memorable, make sure it's in a positive light.

Here's a quick reminder about Takers and other relationship vampires. Do you ever get the feeling you are the only one contributing to a relationship? Or that someone wants to be a part of your world for self-serving reasons? Be watchful for people who are only in the relationship for themselves, even if they appear to be your people at first. Some can play the game really well and make you believe they are powerful, giving contacts. Then, when you least expect it, they hit you with a needy request or create a drama that pulls you in. Watch out for these people – and be sure you don't become one of these parasitic success saboteurs yourself.

Express gratitude regularly and sincerely.

Whether it's simply counting your blessings as a way to energize yourself each day or sending thank you notes to those who have made a difference in your world, showing gratitude and appreciation are excellent ways to energize yourself and your relationships. Who doesn't like being told or reminded of how much or how often they have impacted others? Be sure to let your people know how they have made a special impact on your life or business. It doesn't matter how much time has gone by. It will never get old, and it will give them a glow that few other things can.

The legendary Zig Ziglar suggests going a step further and creating a Wall of Gratitude – a special place where you post photos of the people who have made a positive impact on your life and career. Consider how these people fit into your world today, and don't forget to thank them. Gratitude is one of the most wonderful and healing emotions you can express. It will bring you dividends many times over.

try this!

Create your own Wall of Gratitude or even an album or journal of the special people in your life and what they've done for you. Or give yourself a Gratitude Day where you spend the entire day (or part of it) writing thank you notes or making thank you calls. You will feel absolutely terrific doing this!

I recently sent what I thought would be a relatively small referral to one of my most valued colleagues. The lead turned out to be something very positive and valuable for her and her business. She initially thanked me by phone. A few days later I received a beautiful, handwritten note on her elegant, personalized stationery. In the note, my colleague confirmed how much she valued what I did for her and how much she wants to see me succeed as well. Furthermore, the words she used in her gracious note clarified for me what it is I do best, why it matters, and why it's important for me to get up each day and do what I do. The flow of energy in this exchange could light up Las Vegas.

Recognize others for their accomplishments as well. People love to know you're paying attention when they receive awards, media exposure, or do good works for others. Send out notes to congratulate your people on their latest triumphs.

Along those lines, when you receive awards or recognition, remember to be gracious and humble. Most people know what being gracious means, but some often misunderstand what it means to be humble. It's not about shying away from the spotlight, cowering in the corner, or even deflecting a compliment. Humility is being who you truly are, no more than but also no less than that. There is no reason not to shine and be your best self, but be careful not to become too self-important. Arrogance is not an attractive quality.

Avoid gossip and negativity.

When you are in a conversation, note the purpose, spirit, and tone of the information or exchange. Would you want the person or group you are talking about (or anyone else) to overhear you? Is the discussion productive? Are solutions being discussed? If not, it's probably idle gossip, chatter, or sour grapes.

Once you become aware of how much time and energy people (and the media) spend on gossip, negativity, drama, and other people's problems, you will recognize what an energy-drainer and time-waster it is, and you won't want any part of it. People who engage in this as a regular practice are probably not your people anyway. What's more, any negative or malicious comments you slip into a conversation reflect on you more than anyone. Who needs it?

Honor privacy and confidentiality.

You won't be seen as trustworthy if you reveal information that should remain private. Plus there are client confidentiality rules that govern many professions. Be sure to honor and follow them.

Under-promise and over-deliver.

It's always better to exceed expectations than to disappoint. This can be difficult if you are an enthusiastic, high-energy person who wants to say yes and please others. It's also so easy to over-estimate what you can do when you are caught up in the moment. Hold back just a little when telling others what you can do for them.

* * *

The key to building a reputation of integrity:
say what you'll do, then do what you say.

* * *

allow for change and evolution

Change happens in life, work, and relationships, so know that letting go will happen now and then, and it's okay. You've done your best to stay in touch, do for the other person, and keep a connection you value alive, but you're just not getting any response or reciprocation. Or it's just too much work. Or no longer a mutually valuable fit. If that's the case, it may be time to admit that the relationship is fading away or needs to end. Let it go with grace knowing that if you are meant to get back in touch, you will. And if not, there is an open space that will be filled by someone else. There are seasons and cycles to relationships.

Even if relationships change or end, try not to burn bridges. Sometimes relationships have to come to an end because of disagreements or other breakup-worthy reasons. That will happen now and then. Whenever possible, even if you have to close the bridge, try not to destroy it entirely. Time and distance can sometimes heal whatever issue created the breakup, and civility and respect can reign. What's more, you never know if and when you may need each other again. Be firm, but also gracious and respectful.

However, some bridges need prompt and thorough burning. There may be circumstances where you need to completely, thoroughly, and permanently break away and distance yourself from a relationship that is potentially dangerous, damaging, or otherwise negative – and not much will ever change that.

As you work with or are in touch with those in your Top Contacts database, be sure to keep their information up to date. Add in notes that can help you build the relationship. If someone is no longer worthy of a spot in your Top Contact database, transfer them back to your general database.

The bottom line here is to stay focused on your people; those who make the most positive impact on you, your purpose, and your business. Who brings the most energy and value to your work and life? What relationships are the most mutually rewarding?

why do this work?

Being mindful of who you want to connect and be associated with raises the bar on many levels. The more you appreciate, value, and stay connected to your best people and others like them, the more success, value, and joy you will enjoy in your work and life.

People will get to know you, remember you, and appreciate the characteristics that make you stand above the crowd and make you special. They will "get" you and remember what you're all about. They'll remember that you helped them. You'll have strong, loyal connections that grow over time, and you'll stay connected and informed. People will regard you with respect and become your advocates and ambassadors. This will help you attract more business, opportunities, and connections. And because you've shown that you care about quality and want strong two-way relationships, you'll always be close to the answers, resources, and experts when you need them.

As Jim Cathcart, speaker and author of *The Acorn Principle and Relationship Selling* told me recently, "It's not what you know or who you know that counts. What counts is who is glad that they know *you!*" Which brings us to the next chapter.

CHAPTER 7

⁎ stand out in the crowd

ATTRACTING STRONG RELATIONSHIPS IN GROUP SETTINGS

In this chapter, you will:

- Learn how to select the networking events that are right for you and your business.

- Develop skills that will help you get the most out of events.

- Read expert tips for networking with more intention, polish, and presence.

- Discover how to be more attractive and memorable to others.

Over coffee, Linda and Sue were talking about a business luncheon they had attended the day before. Sue thought the event particularly enjoyable, inspiring, and energizing. She found the speaker fascinating and was pleased with the people who had shown up for the event. She made several new contacts and reconnected with others on her Top Contact list. It had been a fruitful day for Sue and well worth her time.

Sue expected Linda to offer a similar impression of the event, especially since many of the attendees were excellent prospects for Linda's business; several were even existing customers. She was surprised when Linda had a negative view. She reported that she hadn't met anyone interesting, hadn't enjoyed any good conversations, and thought the speaker was boring. Linda left the meeting feeling it was a waste of her time and was considering dropping her membership from the organization.

Sue wondered if it was possible she and Linda had attended the same event. Granted, everyone has a unique perspective regarding a situation, and no two people will have the exact opinion on anything. But as Sue looked back on the event, she saw several possible causes for Linda's disappointment.

First, Linda had been under a lot of stress that week with family and financial issues that could easily put anyone in a negative frame of mind. Second, Linda had shown up at the event thirty minutes late, missing the mix-and-mingle segment of the event. Sue always made sure she was there early enough to enjoy that part of the meeting, when the best connecting occurs. She compared missing it to skipping the warm-up portion of an exercise class. Third, Linda's late entrance meant she had to sit in the only available seat at a table in the back of the room. Linda's chair was positioned so her back was to the podium, where it was hard to see and hear the speaker. Finally, many of Linda's customers and contacts who were at the event never saw Linda because they were at other tables and had to leave when the event was over or were busy conversing with others.

No wonder Sue and Linda had such contrasting experiences! Sue had networked with intention while Linda had just made a haphazard appearance on a day when she wasn't in the best frame of mind. There could have been many other factors at play as well.

networking factors to consider

There is a difference between merely attending and *showing up* at the networking events that are right for you. "Networking" is the term you most likely use when talking about attending events to meet people, make connections, seek opportunities and leads, and get the word out about whatever it is you're doing, selling, promoting, or advocating. Networking doesn't always get the credit it is due. Some people don't bother to network at all and have a number of excuses for this. Some people approach networking carelessly or as an afterthought, without any idea of what they want to get out of it. Some network too aggressively, thinking it's a forum for peddling their wares or having others solve their problems. They actually repel the very people whom they hope to attract.

People likely to fail at networking show a number of typical traits. For example, they:

- ❋ **think networking is all about them.**

- ❋ **believe networking is about selling.**

- ❋ **get impatient or frustrated when it doesn't generate instant results.**

- ❋ **don't make networking a regular and ongoing part of their business.**

* show up only when business is slow or they need something.

* are not strategic, purposeful, or prepared.

* attend events that aren't the right fit for them, their needs, or their goals.

* show up late and leave early.

* lack professionalism, presence, and polish.

* have undeveloped networking and interpersonal skills.

* don't understand how to make the most of a networking event.

* attempt to pursue rather than attract.

* neglect the follow-up stages after making initial connections.

In contrast, people who network well and achieve the most success are the ones who mindfully choose to:

* be mindful givers.

* build relationships first.

* invest in long-term results.

* make networking part of their regular routine.

* show up regularly and consistently.

* be strategic, proactive, and purposeful.

* attend networking events that are a good fit for them.

* arrive at events on time and stay until the end.

✳ learn and consistently practice good networking skills.

✳ be open to learning and meeting new people.

✳ show warm, relaxed attitudes.

✳ make the most of each and every networking event.

✳ allow the laws of attraction to work in their favor.

✳ invest in timely, considerate follow-up

Getting out there is important on many levels. The beauty of attending a business gathering is that it gives you a range of social and learning opportunities all in one place. You can meet, greet, or just observe many different people in one venue and make thoughtful decisions about whether you'd like to get to know them better. It's a place to gather first impressions and collect information. (But be aware: others are doing the same with you.)

: Good networkers seem to have the uncanny ability to spot, attract, and connect with the people they are hoping to meet. Is it luck? Nope. It takes skill, finesse, and practice.

✳ ✳ ✳

Think of networking events as the place where the dance of making business connections begins.

✳ ✳ ✳

When attending events, remember that you are seeking to meet *your people* – the people with whom you may want to build relationships, learn, do business, and exchange resources and referrals. You might have an engaging conversation with someone and know immediately that you would like to get to know them better and possibly do business with them. Or you may have a conversation with someone who just doesn't impress or interest you. You don't resonate with them; they're not your people.

It may sound shallow, but events give you time to shop and compare. They offer the time and space for many interactions and interviews. Keep in mind that, like interviewing someone for a job, you may need to observe and interact with several people, and several times with each, before deciding if they are a fit for you.

* * *

I can't stress this too often: first impressions <u>do</u> matter. Furthermore, first impressions impact subsequent impressions.

* * *

regularity counts

When it comes to networking, connecting, and building long-term relationships, one thing's for sure: you can't win if you don't play. That's why it's important to attend business and networking events on a regular basis, not just when business slows or you need something. To really connect with others and to be memorable over time, networking, following up, and staying in touch must be a regular part of your routine and budget.

Showing up regularly gives others the chance to get to know you and shows consistency and dedication on your part. People like these traits. People do business with people they know and trust. Showing up regularly and networking strategically and thoughtfully helps with both. It also makes you more memorable; others may think of you first if and when they need your services, expertise, or products.

Networking isn't just about sales.

Some people measure the value and ROI of attending networking and business events regularly only in terms of how many leads they get and how these efforts immediately impact sales. That's a short-sighted way to view the investment of your time and money. There is so much more to be gained from attending networking events regularly.

For starters, the people you want to meet aren't just your potential customers. They are also the people who might become affiliates, advisors, mentors, ambassadors and advocates who spread the word about you or refer business to you, brainstorming partners, and other colleagues of value.

Networking events are also forums for hearing industry news and expanding your knowledge. Many events include expert speakers, panels, and other types of professional development programs. Being a life-long learner open to picking up new skills, hearing about trends and best practices, and considering new points of view and perspectives has long been key to success.

Still, many people use excuses for not networking regularly. These excuses include:

- ⁂ **It's boring.**

- ⁂ **It's too time-consuming.**

- ⁂ **I'm too busy.**

- ⁂ **It's too expensive.**

- ⁂ **It never pays off.**

- ⁂ **I don't enjoy it.**

- ⁂ **I'm too shy.**

❋ It feels awkward to be around people I don't know.

❋ It disrupts my schedule/day/productivity.

❋ I don't know which events or groups are right for me/my business.

❋ I never meet anyone worthwhile.

❋ The people I meet are rude and always trying to sell me something.

❋ I don't know what to wear.

❋ I don't know what to do once I get there.

❋ I get too busy and I forget.

Maybe some of these reasons resonate with you. But the reasons to network regularly and strategically outweigh them a hundredfold. It is critical to your long-term business growth, and is a powerful and productive investment if done strategically and properly. It can also be enjoyable and energizing once you know who your people are and how and where to connect with them. If nothing else, it can be an excellent way to get you out of the office, give you a much-needed break, and allow you to see the bigger picture. And the more you do it and educate yourself on how to do it, the more you will enjoy it.

which events to attend?

Being strategic and purposeful, even selective, about which events you attend is the next step. This is where you will find great economy in terms of your time and money; as well as improve your chances of seeing positive, if not a dramatic improvement in overall results.

The first step is to do your research and gather information about the many events to consider attending. You can do this via several methods. For example, you can ask trusted friends and colleagues. You can also check local news and business media listings, social media, and online resources and websites. Begin by searching for organizations and events that focus on your field of work or are venues where you believe you are likely to find your people.

> Networking groups evolve and venues change. The leadership teams change. New groups and events will continue to pop up. Keeping up with what's happening on the networking scene should be part of your news gathering on an ongoing basis.

Be strategic and purposeful, but also be prepared to experiment. Be open to possibilities, try out several organizations and events, and perhaps attend some events several times. You'll eventually discover which events and organizations feel like the best fit for you.

Develop your networking criteria by strategically mapping what you want out of the networking events and gatherings you attend and the groups you choose to belong to. This not only makes attending events and gatherings more efficient, effective, and rich with long-term potential, it also can make the task of networking more energizing and enjoyable.

Here are some questions that can jumpstart the process of identifying events that are the best fit for you. These questions can also help you determine how to best fit networking into your regular schedule. Feel free to add more questions to those suggested, or delete others that don't matter to you. You'll want to customize this list to your needs and preferences.

purpose

✳ **What is the purpose, objective, or theme of the organization or event? Networking? Business development? Lead sharing? Learning? Fundraising? Celebrating an event?**

✳ **Does this interest you?**

✳ **Is this a good fit for your business efforts?**

✳ **Does the group demonstrate a philosophy that encourages attendees to be givers rather than merely takers?**

the people who attend

✳ **Will this event be attended by the type and caliber of people you wish to meet? Potential customers or clients? Peers or potential mentors from whom you can learn or be inspired? People who have experiences you wish to model and learn from?**

✳ **At what types of events have you met your people in the past? Is this a similar type of event? Note traits and patterns of those events and use them to guide you. Does it have a history of attracting top-notch people and your Top 20%?**

host/organizer

✳ **Is the event hosted or sponsored by a reputable person, team, or organization known for putting on high-quality, well-regarded, and well-attended events?**

✳ **Does the host or host organization have a clear vision and mission statement, and solid leadership?**

programs and learning opportunities

❈ **Does this group or event offer programs, speakers, or learning opportunities of interest and value to you?**

❈ **Is the speaker at a specific event someone you want to hear or possibly meet? Or is the speaker someone you already know and wish to support?**

❈ **Is the program topic an area where you wish to broaden your knowledge or improve your skills?**

❈ **Will this program attract people whom you want to meet and be around?**

❈ **Does the program allow for some unstructured mingling time?**

time/date/location

❈ **Do the date, time, and location work with your schedule and typical routine?**

❈ **Is the location and setting appealing?**

❈ **How will the type of meeting, time, day, and location affect who shows up and why?**

frequency and time commitment

❈ **Does this event seem worth fitting into your schedule?**

❈ **How many events can you realistically and sustainably attend per week or month?**

❈ **Should this event be one of them?**

❈ **Which events and organizations are on your top priority list and why?**

financial commitment

❄ How much are you willing to invest in membership and registration fees for events?

❄ If the fees for this event or organization are high, will it be worth it? Will it weed out those who are not serious about their businesses? Or just be a big expense?

❄ If an event is free, what does that mean? Who will that event attract? Will it still be worth the investment of my valuable time? Events with dollar requirements are often attended by people who are serious about their business. Free events can be valuable, however "free" often attracts people who are simply looking for, well, something for free.

leadership/volunteer commitment

❄ Are you able to serve on a committee or in a leadership position for the organization?

❄ Would there be value to you in doing so?

❄ Would you learn something you want to learn through this experience?

❄ Would you be able to work with people you want to know better?

❄ Would it help you give back, demonstrate your skills and talents, and strengthen your brand?

❄ Would it help you gain needed experience as well as visibility?

Some thoughts on after-hours events.

Some networking events take place after hours, including happy hours, cocktail receptions and mixers, dinners, and evening programs. These provide an excellent way to relax, unwind, and interact with others after a long day. But do consider that many of these gatherings involve alcohol, which can affect the level of professionalism at the event.

Happy hours can be joyous, celebratory, energizing, and fun. They can help people "get real" and bond. They can also be unpleasant, crowded, loud, unproductive, and even disastrous to your reputation if you over-imbibe. They sometimes attract young professionals and singles, some of whom haven't yet modified their college socializing habits.

Finally, if you are among people who are stressed-out or unhappy, after-hours events can become nothing more than venting or ad hoc therapy sessions. Nothing wrong with letting off steam or listening to someone who needs a friend, but be mindful of whom you do this with and what you say, as well as when, where, and how often. Some of your dark secrets and insecurities are best kept to yourself or shared with a trusted confidante or trained professional.

> Lots of factors to consider here, so plan wisely to ensure that the events you attend are suitable, enjoyable, energizing, and productive for you.

recognizing quality events

If you want to spend every waking hour attending professional events and other gatherings where you might meet potentially valuable colleagues and customers, most urban areas could provide you with a full roster of events that would make that dream possible. But for most of us, it's not realistic or desirable. Some of us are lucky if we can get to one or two meetings a week or month. And that's okay. There is no need to attend every event, join every organization, or even accept every invitation extended to you, especially if you have developed a clear list of criteria to help you choose the events that are best for you.

> True story: I began getting particular and strategic about the events I attended after visiting a leads group where one attendee came up to me and announced that if I wasn't going to bring him leads, I wasn't welcome back. Who needs that kind of warm welcome?

Consider the secret of many successful people: raise your standards. Get fussy and particular. Go for what puts you in touch with the level and caliber of people you want to meet. Also go for venues and scenarios that allow you the opportunity to really get to know these people and stay in contact with them. Trade quantity for quality in your networking efforts.

I've discovered that sometimes the best places for meeting high-quality people are in smaller, more intimate settings. For example, my friends Anne Lasseigne Tiedt, a public relations expert and speaker who co-owns Momentum Public Relations, and Marny Lifshen, communications expert, speaker, and author of *Some Assembly Required: A Networking Guide for Women*, had the brilliant idea to host an exclusive, invitation-only, after-hours gathering in a private room at a local bistro. They each invited a dozen carefully selected colleagues and contacted them personally by phone and well in advance, to be sure they could save the date. Those who were invited saw how much care Anne and Marny took to orchestrate this exclusive event. As a result, nearly all the invitees made it a priority to attend.

We gathered, mingled, sipped wine, and sampled delicious, beautifully presented appetizers. We engaged in interesting, memorable conversations. It was so pleasant, natural, productive, and energizing. I felt honored to be among those invited and had a fabulous time.

Several colleagues I value were there, and I had ample time to reconnect with each of them. In addition, I met several new people, all of whom I promptly added to my database, which I don't do very often.

Inspired by Anne and Marny, I later co-hosted a similar event for a friend who had just written and published a book. Twelve amazing women gathered over good food and conversation in a mutual friend's lovely home while our friend, the newly published author, told us stories of her publishing journey. It was a celebration as well as a great way to connect and reconnect with other like-minded people.

Another colleague told me that a local networking group she belongs to just launched a special interest group (SIG) created for members who have been solopreneurs for five years or more. This allows them to spend concentrated time with peers who have comparable experience levels. It also gives the general membership something to look forward to as they continue on their entrepreneurial journey and reach the same level of experience.

Members from yet another professional group launched their own book club. They read and gather to discuss a designated business book each month. Other friends belong to mastermind groups and wisdom circles that meet regularly.

Yet another colleague has reintroduced the concept of the Salon, which is essentially the art and science of gathering interesting friends and colleagues together to share great ideas, discuss pre-selected topics, and indulge in superb conversation.

Expand your reach beyond your community.

Local events may be the most convenient and affordable way to make networking part of your regular routine, but also consider attending regional, national, and international events in other cities as well, perhaps once or twice a year. These larger scale events can bring you broader perspectives on your business and industry, the latest information on best practices, connections with high-level experts and leaders in your field, and world-class programs and speakers. Plus these conferences get you out of your typical environment.

* * *

While searching for the best networking venues, consider also the benefits of attending regional and national events.

* * *

Experiment, give it time, keep notes, and make adjustments.

Give your search for the best networking venues and opportunities some time and patience. Realize that finding groups and events that feel right to you may take a little time and involve some trial and error. You may have to attend an organization's event several times before you know if it's right for you. Many things, from the date and time to the speaker and program, can affect the event and impact who shows up. Whom you see and what you experience the first time may vary from that of another visit. Also consider that a group that seems like a perfect fit today, may not be the right fit in a few years. Needs change. Standards evolve.

Be observant and talk to people you know and trust. Ask people in your Top 20% what events they attend and why. What new organization or upcoming event seems like the place to be? Pay attention to these bits of intelligence. You'll find that good people are where good people gather.

preparing for networking success

Once you decide to attend an event – because it's a fit for you, others have recommended it, or you're simply going to give it a try – bring yourself to the next level and prepare for the experience. Start by developing your intentions before you even set foot out the door.

Here's a Networking with Intention exercise that can help you walk into any gathering primed and ready to tune into the people, connections, information, resources, and experiences you are seeking. It doesn't have to take but a few minutes and you will find it amazingly effective.

Step 1 - Be descriptive.

On a sheet of paper or note card, create a list of words and phrases that describe the experience you want from the event. You can go to a website such as wordle.net to create a word cloud if that suits you. Your words may include some of these: Effortless – Enjoyable – Friendly – Productive – Stimulating – Inspiring – Engaging – Worthwhile – Educational – Warm – Welcoming – Fun. Really think about what would make this event a great experience for you. What words would describe it if it were so?

Step 2 - Compose your intentions.

Now make a second list of what you intend to receive, attract, learn, or experience at the networking event you are about to attend. Keep it simple, open, and not overly specific. These aren't concrete, measurable goals; they are intentions, which are broader in scope. Leave some of the details up to synchronicity. Don't limit yourself or put constraints on the possibilities. For example, your intentions might be as follows – "I intend to:

- ❉ **Meet and connect with interesting new people who understand and value my experience and services/products.**

- ❉ **Meet and connect with someone who has an important piece of information to share with me.**

- ❉ **Share information about a new product or promotion my business now offers with someone who wants and needs to hear about it.**

- ❉ **Attract a valuable new colleague, advisor, or client.**

- ❉ **Learn something new that can make a positive difference in my business/projects.**

- ❉ **Be open to a piece of advice I need to hear today.**

- ❉ **Be inspired and rejuvenated.**

- ❉ **Receive a powerful new idea.**

- ❉ **Reconnect with people I haven't seen in awhile.**

- ❉ **Be open to hearing, learning, or experiencing that which I need most in my business.**

These are just samples. Write down what your intentions are. What do you need for your business? Beyond just more sales and customers?

Step 3 - Determine your priorities.

Once you have your list of intentions, place a star next to the three to five intentions that are most important to you.

Step 4 - Review the list.

Depending on your personal preference, review the list one more time and put it away, or put the list in your wallet or purse for handy reference and ongoing inspiration.

Step 5 - Show up and watch what happens.

You've actually "programmed" a part of your brain, the Reticular Activating System (RAS). The RAS filters all incoming stimuli and helps you decide whether to notice or ignore something. Now your job is to show up while your RAS helps you "tune in" to whom and what you're seeking. Then take appropriate action.

Step 6 - Review and compare.

After the event, review your list and see how your words and intentions compare with the actual experience. Prepare to be amazed.

This exercise can be applied to many parts of your business and life. It's one of the secrets on which many successful people rely.

try this!

If you forgot to do the previous exercise, try this quick version while on your way to the event. (But remember your number one task is to get there safely!) Turn off your phone, the music, and as many other distractions as safely possible. Let a little silence set in. Try to relax and breathe slowly and deeply. If you're excited about the event, that's okay. Just try not to stress (if you can do some deep breathing, stress will actually transform into exhilaration). Ponder the event you are attending. Ask yourself, "Why did I decide to attend this event today? What do I want to experience or attract? Whom do I want to see and meet?"

See what pops into your head. Sometimes it may be something as simple as, "I want to see my friends and colleagues and connect with one or two new people," or "I want to learn some new things that will help me take my business to the next level." You might even realize that you're not quite sure why you're going or what you want, but you are ready and open for it to be a positive experience.

My colleague Rita was on her way to an event one day and practiced the above exercise. While in her car she tried to come up with three intentions, but was only able to think of two. "I stopped forcing the matter," she says, "and I realized my third intention was merely to keep an open mind and watch for something totally unexpected but positive to happen." At the event, Rita found herself sitting next to someone with precisely the expertise she needed to create a new website with the special features she wanted. Mission accomplished!

try this!

Create a positive attraction mantra. Before you enter an event, simply create a positive statement that will be your theme. Be as open or as specific as you feel you need to be.

Professional writer and editor Hope J. Lafferty used this one at an event she attended: "I am drawn to people who will lead me to the projects, clients, information, and results that are right for me."

If you're more spiritual, compose a simple prayer such as this one: "May God/the Universe /my Trusted Source open my eyes, ears, mind, and heart today. May I attract and be open to the people I am meant to meet and the lessons, messages, and inspirations I am meant to hear."

The time you take to set your intentions or visualize what you want can be a very relaxing and enjoyable time. Taking even one or two minutes to do some of these activities can help you be more prepared and at ease and will help you enter an event feeling fresh, calm, at your best, purposeful, and feeling receptive.

Make these exercises a regular habit – and watch what happens!

understand and leverage the power of presence

Create positive first impressions and project your brand – always. Whenever you're at meetings or gatherings, or even just out in public during the work week, it pays to be well-groomed, well-dressed, put together, and feeling your best. Picture yourself stepping inside the neighborhood coffee shop for a latte on a Tuesday morning in your workout attire with no make-up and a scowl on your face because you just had an argument with your teenager. It never fails – the less put-together you are and the more ornery you feel, the more likely you'll run into an important client, colleague, or contact. I've learned my lesson on that one!

Remember who you are and what you're seeking. Are you projecting the image and brand that aligns with these? Let this be your guide as you make decisions about how to present yourself, conduct yourself, communicate, and interact with others. If you don't "show up" in a manner congruent with what you say you want or how you describe yourself to others, you are guilty of sending mixed messages, which will quickly erode your credibility and integrity. And forget any possibility of attracting what you say you want.

Here are some power and presence tips that will maximize your chances of successfully showing up in integrity with who you are.

Adopt a positive frame of mind.

The best and first business strategy you can adopt – and the one that costs the least – is a conscious choice to maintain and project a positive attitude, especially when you are out and about. This timeless success strategy is mentioned in countless books, articles, and programs on how to achieve success in life and in business. Attitude matters, so choose a good one. Does it mean you have to walk around looking like a puppet with a fake smile? No, but if you work at adjusting your thoughts and feel grateful for what's going right in your life, the smile and positive will surface. It's something you have to work at and practice.

What if you have an event on your calendar and you're not feeling well or simply having a bad day? If it's not mandatory that you attend an event or step out the door, don't go. Call in sick and get some rest. Do whatever it is you do to make yourself feel better. It's okay to accept that it's not a good day for you to be out and "on." If you must cancel an event to which you sent an RSVP, be sure to contact the host or event organizer, apologize, and let them know you will not be there. (Be prepared that you may not receive a refund.)

On the other hand, if you need to show up, it's time to summon whatever energy you can possibly muster, pull yourself together, get there, and be as close to 100% as possible. Busy professionals, celebrities, community leaders, newscasters, and other public figures pull this off every day. You can too. If the show must go on, then on with the show.

I've had to do this on a number of occasions. One of the best efforts I ever made was when I had to give a presentation to a group of professional women while suffering a terrible allergy attack. I was on three different medications and my head felt like a weather balloon. I was lapsing between drowsy and hyper, a little light-headed, and my voice sounded more like Lauren Bacall's than my own. Yet I put on my best suit, a vivid silk blouse, and my most stylish and energizing accessories. I used every makeup trick in the book to look credible, attractive, rested, and healthy. I envisioned a good hair day, took an EmergenC®, prepared a thermos of tea with honey and lemon, and got in the car. On the way, I played the happiest, most upbeat music I could find, thought happy thoughts, and prayed.

I admit that when I got to the event location, I went to the ladies room, looked in the mirror and asked myself, "What are you doing? How on earth are you going to pull this off?"

But once I began my presentation, gained a little momentum, and tapped into my desire to deliver a good presentation to my audience, I was able to sail through it. One of my most successful and discerning colleagues was in the front row. She later told me it was one of the best presentations she'd seen me give. I wondered how it could be so. A speaking coach later told me it was probably because I was "real" with my audience and myself, yet did everything I could to do a good job and not disappoint them.

* * *

In the end, life is never perfect. Sometimes you just have to show up and give it a little extra effort. This is what separates the good from the great.

* * *

It's worth saying again: dress appropriately.

Still think that appearance doesn't matter and that you should be judged for what's on the inside? Okay. Then think about how you feel when you've invested in yourself and your appearance and you know you are showing up looking great. How does that feel? Pretty terrific, right? Do you suppose feeling good, confident, and prepared will affect how others perceive and respond to you? You bet. End of argument.

Don't try to fake it or tell yourself, "Oh, I'll just show up casual today." If it's considered acceptable to show up at a luncheon in a sweater and slacks (and that's how everyone else is usually dressed), be bold and different. Take your attire up a notch and wear a jacket or suit with a collared blouse and some tasteful accessories. You don't have to dress in an over-the-top manner or don a black suit for every outing, but be one whose attire and presence says, "I'm a true professional. I'm serious about my business and being successful. I have it together. I know what I'm doing. You can rely on me."

Are you one of these painful examples?

Painful Example A: A gentleman who owns a financial planning firm shows up at a networking event wearing jeans, a Hawaiian shirt, and sandals. His reasoning for this attire: "It's summertime. This is what's comfortable to me." The messages he is sending: "I would rather be on vacation or lounging by the pool than working on my clients' financials." Or "My comfort means more to me than my clients and my business." My money is staying where it is, thank you.

Painful Example B: A college graduate seeking her first "real job" attends a professional event wearing a mini skirt, a tight t-shirt that says "Sweet" across her bosom, and a bright orange velour hoodie. She is carrying a Gucci purse. This woman is hoping to find a mentor and gather some job leads. Her reasoning for her attire: "I don't have anything else to wear." The messages she is sending: "I would rather be back in college, at the mall, or on Spring Break. Mom and Dad pay for everything, but have not taught me anything about the real world. I have no clue how to earn or spend my money wisely. I am not that interested in my career or my future." Would you bother to ask for this woman's resume, let alone take the time to interview her?

Painful Example C: A photographer shows up at an event where the program topic is "How to Attract Referrals to Higher Paying Clients." He is wearing worn jeans, a dirty, wrinkled shirt, and a beat-up leather jacket. His hair is greasy, long, and unkempt. He is sporting at least three days' worth of untrimmed beard growth. He is carrying a tattered canvas backpack – and a very expensive camera with a huge, expensive lens. The speaker talks about the importance of first impressions, image, attire, grooming, and overall appearance in attracting higher paying clients. She gives the audience tips for updating and upgrading their wardrobes and personal brands. The photographer scoffs, rolls his eyes, and argues throughout the presentation. He complains that people like him can't possibly spend that kind of money on work clothes. He has bills to pay and a wife and infant son to support. Message he is sending: "I care more about my opinions, my photography equipment, and playing the role of starving artist than my success, my clients, and my ability to provide for my family." Would you hire this man and have him involved in a project with your best client?

Bottom line: It *does* matter how you present yourself.

Be on time.

Show up on time, perhaps even a bit early. Somehow we have been bamboozled into thinking it's glamorous to be fashionably late. Granted, the unexpected phone call hits, an emergency arises, or traffic is ridiculously snarled more than usual. Or perhaps you are someone who networks a lot, receives many invitations, has to make the rounds, and attempts to be in two places at one time. Sometimes it's just not possible to arrive at an event right as it is beginning. It happens.

If networking tardiness is a regular habit due to poor planning, however, it can hurt you in the long run. Being on time makes a statement all its own. It demonstrates that you want to be there, pay attention to details, know how to manage your schedule and time, and respect and value others' time as well. Showing up late means you could miss out on some of the best networking opportunities. You also can't enter an event calmly and ready to meet people if you are stressed out and harried, and your tardiness may disrupt a program in progress or distract others. Be punctual whenever possible.

Be prepared.

Always bring along professional business cards. It drives me crazy when someone is willing to spend the time and money to attend a business event, but when in the midst of a connection and asked for their card, they come up with a lame excuse along the lines of, "Oh, I left those at home," or "Oh darn they are in my other purse," or "Uh … I haven't had time to print any."

Another pet peeve is when people hand me their card and it looks like an afterthought – badly designed, crumpled, amateurish, or impossible to read without a magnifying glass.

To make the best impression, make sure your business cards are in your purse or pocket at all times. They should be protected in an attractive, professional business card case; professionally designed, produced and printed to reflect and reinforce your desired brand and image; printed on high-quality card stock (no perforated edges); readable and with the information others need to reach you; and something that people will want to save, not toss in the circular file.

Some additional notes on business card etiquette: when handing your card to someone, be sure it is facing up and toward them. When someone hands you their card, take a moment to look at it. These little things show you care and that others matter to you.

> Every day, wherever you go, you are in some way, shape, or form presenting yourself to the world, "interviewing" for your next job, or attracting (or repelling) your next great client.

be mindful of others and conduct yourself with professionalism and polish

Jan Goss, business etiquette expert, founder of Civility Consulting and the Austin School of Protocol, and author of *Protocol Power: 21 Days to Professional Polish,* generously shares these basic tips you can use to polish up your business etiquette skills, put others at ease (which is what etiquette is really about), rise above the crowd, out-class your competition, and be memorable in any business setting.

As with some of the other tips you've read in this chapter, much of what Jan suggests is all about what you do before you arrive at the event.

"Being polished starts with becoming mentally, emotionally, and physically prepared," says Jan. "There are no short cuts to doing the internal work. It's about becoming centered and grounded, putting yourself in the right frame of mind, and most of all thinking of others and showing respect always."

Jan Goss' top tips for being the most polished, courteous person in the room:

* *Remember: it's not about you.*

* **Remind yourself of #1 as often as possible.**

* **As you get out of your car, approach the building, and enter any event, think of the words "glide" or "smooth." This simple trick helps you move more confidently and gracefully.**

* **Smile.**

* **Nervous or stressed? Think of the word "great." It will shift your thoughts and emotions. Notice how your facials muscles change. Don't be surprised if you find yourself smiling.**

* **Be mindful of your posture. Stand tall, chin up, eyes bright, chest up, shoulders back and down.**

* **Place your hands at your sides, along the seam of your jacket, slacks, or skirt. This feels funny at first, but you'll look confident, relaxed, and natural, not fidgety or uneasy.**

* **In any setting, act as if you belong – because you do!**

* Be attentive to others. Look them in the eyes and smile. Listen thoughtfully.

* Use "Hello" instead of "Hi" when greeting others. This shows far more respect, attentiveness, and warmth.

* Add another dose of warmth by adding a second greeting, as in "Hello, good morning" or "Hello, good afternoon."

* Go for the trifecta by adding in the person's name: "Hello, good morning, Ann." "Hello, good evening, Jim." Watch what happens. People will react to this with similar warmth and friendliness.

* When introducing yourself follow this formula: "Hello" + [your name] + [your company name]. As in, "Hello. Deborah Anderson. Anderson Consulting Company."

* Know that it's *your* responsibility to introduce yourself at professional functions. Don't wait for others to approach you or to make introductions.

* When introducing yourself, look for people standing alone or groups of three or more. This prevents the faux pas of interrupting conversations in progress.

* Learn and practice the elements of a good handshake:

  • Extend your hand from your elbow.

  • Keep your hand open and flat – not cupped or crumpled.

  • Connect with the other person by meeting hands, web-to-web (that's the spot between your thumb and forefinger).

- **Clasp the other person's hand firmly, but gently (no bone crushing!)**

- **Shake twice, no more than three times, from the elbow, not from the shoulder.**

- **Release.**

- **This sounds simple, but actually takes practice to do it correctly.**

A few more notes about handshakes - it's startling how many people, even some of the most seasoned professionals, do not shake hands properly. Be aware that many handshake variations express an equal number of body language messages, many of them negative. Hesitant. Shy. Disinterested. Controlling. Condescending. Nervous. The list is long. Once you know the right way, you'll notice this as well. Get your handshake in shape beginning now!

Remember names.

This one can be difficult, especially if you know a lot of people or are working on projects that make it feel like your head is ready to explode. Nevertheless, strive to use and remember names whenever possible. It's a talent that makes others feel good and is worth cultivating. Studies have shown that everyone's favorite word (even if they don't freely admit it) is their name. Here are some quick tips for remembering names.

※ **Be mindful of how important this skill is to your success.**

※ **Adjust your attitude: decide you *will* do a better job of remembering names.**

* Make it a top priority to pay attention to people's names.

* Repeat the person's name when you are introduced. (As in, "Hello, David. It's so nice to meet you. So, David, what brings you here today?)

* Use word association or visualization techniques to help you remember (but be cautious here as these can backfire)!

* Don't hesitate to humbly and courteously ask someone to remind you of their name.

Many more techniques are available via classes, in books, and online. Invest in them as they will help you with the important task of remembering others' names. Don't skimp on this.

conversing and connecting

Whenever possible, connect on a personal level and establish rapport before bringing up business. There is nothing wrong with exploring how you can do business with others. In fact, professional reasons are ultimately why you've chosen to attend most networking events. Still, it's vital to remember that business conversations should take place after an initial period of establishing rapport and getting to know each other. This is the secret to creating meaningful, valuable, win-win relationships.

After all, would you ask someone to marry you only a few minutes after meeting them? Of course not! You'd first decide if you liked the person (and they liked you). Then you'd decide if you wanted to see them again and vice versa. Then there would be a period of courtship – typically months and sometimes years. You get the idea. Yes, it's much like dating.

If you want to get to know someone on a better and higher level, ask questions about them as people first, such as, *What brought you here? How did you hear about this event? Have you been here before? Do you know any of the people here?* Remember these simple, high-attraction tips:

* ❊ **Smile.**

* ❊ **Be interested, not interesting.**

* ❊ **Listen more than you talk.**

* ❊ **Be patient, not pushy.**

* ❊ **Be conversational, but not invasive or overly talkative.**

* ❊ **Remember it's not about you.**

* ❊ **Be grateful and gracious.**

Repellent networking behavior: three examples of what not to do.

1. Let's network! Right now! Nothing screams "Run away!" more than the person who only shows up when they need to boost their business and have nothing else on their mind than themselves and their own desperate needs.

I hosted a relatively small invitation-only gathering designed to help some of my favorite people meet and spend time with one another. One of the invitees asked me, graciously and well in advance, if she could bring along a friend. I hesitated at first because I had carefully crafted the guest list and it was invitation-only. In a weak moment, I said yes.

When my friend and her guest arrived at my event, I greeted them and showed them in. They were hardly in the door ten seconds when my friend's guest began asking me questions that felt scripted. I sensed it was a lead-up to a sales pitch about her company and its products. Turns out, I was right! It was neither the time nor the place to begin a conversation of this nature. I was still greeting other guests as they arrived and the nature of the gathering was more social than business. I tried to change the subject and was greeting other arriving guests, but she kept on talking. I finally told her I had to excuse myself to attend to my guests. She finally got the message. I admit it: I avoided her the rest of the evening. In fact, I still avoid her.

Don't be this person. And think carefully on whom you invite to events and whom you bring along as your guests. Their behavior will impact the event and reflect on you.

2. The shock and (non-)awe method. I was seven months pregnant and had just arrived at a holiday luncheon hosted by one of the professional organizations to which I belong. I got there a little early and was enjoying a moment to myself and some refreshments (in my condition I was always hungry and thirsty). As I glanced around the room I spotted a woman who had the solid reputation of networking only when she was desperate for work or clients. Plus her mode of operation was to network in a notoriously annoying and aggressive manner.

So there I was with a glass of water in one hand and a plate of snacks in the other when this woman charged over to me with her hand extended as if she was going to let fly a karate chop.

"Patti DeNucci!" she screeched. "I'm so glad you are here! I've been waiting to meet you! I need to network with you!" I nearly dropped both my plate and glass in order to protect my unborn child from this woman's advances. It took some skillful and evasive moves, but I was able to extract myself from her clutches. Needless to say I never did network (or work) with her then. Nor will I ever. Do you blame me?

3. The block and tackle method. Years later, a similar experience occurred. I had just spoken at a professional event (ironically, on the topic of how to graciously and carefully build long-lasting business relationships and attract referrals) and was collecting my notes, folding up my easel, packing up my briefcase, and preparing to leave. As I was doing this a man I didn't know leapt in front of me, blocking my exit. He shoved a business card at me and began a long-winded, ego-driven introduction on who he was, why he was the greatest at what he did, and why he thought we should have coffee, do business, and create an alliance to conquer the world.

Sure, it was flattering to be approached, but the way he did it was ungracious, forceful, and downright creepy. It was clear he'd not heard a word I'd said in my talk. After several painful minutes, I excused myself. When I got back to my office, I dug his business card out of my pocket and ceremoniously threw it in the trash. Finito.

Further, I've not been back to that organization's meetings for fear of running into that character again.

When's it's time to talk about business.

Be prepared and purposeful. After you have established a rapport, then the inevitable question will arise – what do you do? At this point, it's your cue to describe who you are, what you do, who you serve, and how they benefit. You might add why you enjoy what you do.

At one event I spoke with a woman who was looking for a new job. When I asked her what she was looking for, she said, "Oh, pretty much anything." I think she believed her response would help her appear more open and willing to take on any challenge. Yet to me, her answer revealed a lack of vision, focus, and commitment. By leaving her options wide open, she also risked being extremely unmemorable. It's typically easier for others to help you and point you in the direction of opportunity when you are focused and can articulate your specific needs clearly to others. Don't make others guess what you want.

* * *

Be clear on who you are, what you bring to the table, and what you're seeking.

* * *

This brings us again to the self-introduction or "thirty second elevator speech," as it is often known. As a former advertising copywriter, I appreciate catchy and memorable words, phrases, slogans, and taglines. However, when people try to be too clever or practiced, it can quickly move into canned-and-corny territory. In both cases, it just seems like you're trying too hard. Not attractive.

My rule is you don't have to be catchy or elaborate. You simply need to start with using descriptive terms about who you are, what you do, what challenges you solve, who you serve, and what makes you unique. Clear and sincere. And if it's necessary or preferable to vary how you describe yourself and your business, product, or service, that's great. Different people are going to react differently to different words and phrases. Your job is to make note of what you've said that creates a positive or interested reaction or prompts further questioning and conversation. Keep experimenting until you find what works.

And if you're not sure what's working, try asking someone to explain back to you who you are and what you do. If they hit the target, you've done your job. If not, it might be time to try something different. Keep it original, simple, timely, and meaningful. What can you say about yourself and what you do that wakes people up? What will prompt questions and the start of a great conversation?

strategic arrival tips

When you arrive at an event – on time or a little early – scan the name tags at the registration table. Note who will be at the event. See if you recognize any of the names and make mental notes of the people you want to meet or reconnect with.

Mingle first if there's time. If the event includes a meal, you can select your seat by putting your coat, portfolio, or another personal item on the seat. Don't plunk down at the table immediately if others are standing and visiting. Take advantage of this "free ranging" time to mingle, observe, and make connections and conversation.

If you're a little uneasy, warm up first. Find someone you know and have a brief conversation with them. This can help you get into the flow and mood of the event and become more comfortable. These initial conversations also can lead to introductions and more con- versations. In some cases, if you mention to the host that you don't know anyone else attending, the person may oblige and help you get introduced. Don't make any assumptions here. Remember that in business etiquette it's your responsibility to introduce yourself.

If it's a sit-down event without designated seating, be strategic about choosing a seat. When possible, choose a seat at the table near the podium and facing the speaker, if there is one. You'll not only get an up-close view of the speaker, you may also get to meet the speaker, board members, leaders of the hosting organization, and others who chose deliberately to position themselves in this part of the room. (Getting a good seat is another reason to show up early.)

If everyone is still mingling and you want to find a spot to sit, look for a spot next to someone who has reserved their place with a high quality purse or portfolio. It doesn't have to be high fashion or designer name brand; simply something professional and polished.

People who care about their image and accessories tend to care about their businesses as well.

it's all about being civil and courteous to others

Honor your own personal connecting style.

Some people are extroverts who love meeting lots of people and can "work the room" with great charisma and success. Others are more comfortable engaging in deeper conversations with a much smaller number of people. Be aware of your preference, honor it, and use it to your best advantage. Also consider that your intentions, connecting style, and energy levels will vary from day to day and so will your corresponding mingling strategy. At the same time, honor others' connecting styles. Be mindful of how others connect and strive to be courteous and thoughtful of their styles.

Try having fewer, but more meaningful conversations.

Generally it's better in the long run to make three to five excellent connections than to have twenty shallow, meaningless, and unmemorable glad-handing interactions. If you want to meet and say hello to a lot of people and a particular event is your opportunity, by all means go for it. But don't wander the room promoting your business or wares or you'll only be remembered as a peddler, not a person.

Feeling shy, awkward, or nervous?

Find someone who is standing alone and strike up a conversation. You'll most likely be remembered for being thoughtful, kind, and welcoming. I vividly remember attending a book launch event for a recently published friend. I knew no one in the room but introduced myself to my friend's editor and her husband (who also knew no one). After a few moments of delightful conversation, the editor was obliged to mingle around the room, but her husband and I continued our visit. I was grateful for his company and he mine.

Don't be clingy; divide and conquer.

Attending the event with a friend or colleague? Or spot someone you know? Unless you are there purely to enjoy each other's company, don't stay attached at the hip. You won't meet anyone new and it can appear cliquey to others. Split up. You can regroup later to introduce each other to the people you've had the pleasure to meet.

Err on the friendly side.

If you're not sure if you've met someone before, but they indicate they know you, err on the friendly side and say, "Of course! So great to see you again." Similarly, don't make others feel badly about forgetting your name. There's a woman I run into now and then who I remember only as The Woman Who Made Me Feel Badly for Forgetting Her Name. I had not seen her in two years and when I ran into her at a gathering, I distinctly remembered her, but drew a desperate blank on her name. She instantly said with a hint of scorn, "You never remember my name." I apologized profusely, but every time she sees me she reminds me of my faux pas. I certainly remember her name now, but not in a way that makes we want to get within ten feet of her. Forgive and forget (the faux pas, that is).

Worth repeating: be interested not interesting.

Conversations should be more about the other person than about you. People love to be listened to, heard, and respected. By letting others talk about themselves, you actually become more thoughtful, attractive, and memorable.

Don't try to be the smartest, loudest, or funniest person in the room.

This makes you look insecure and becomes annoying, embarrassing, and old rather quickly. Remember that it's not about you. Don't dominate anyone's time or the conversation. Start by listening and asking what you can do for them. Then chat for a few moments, and move on graciously.

Don't blow anyone off.

There may be instances when you are talking to someone and you see another person you need to talk to. If so, excuse yourself as graciously as possible. Don't under any circumstances make the other person feel as though they weren't interesting enough to keep you engaged in conversation.

Relax, be authentic, and be yourself.

Connecting isn't about "selling" or impressing others. It's about being you, being courteous and thoughtful, and building sincere, lasting, win-win relationships. Have fun with it. Show appreciation. If you don't have the opportunity to do so when you arrive, don't leave the event without thanking the host or representative of the hosting organization for putting on the event. Feel free to thank the speaker or panelists as well. They love to know their contribution to the event had value. What's more, they can become great contacts.

Be humble if you are just getting back into the networking circuit.

If you've been absent from the networking scene and are trying to reconnect with people you have not seen in awhile, be suitably humble about it, and bring others up to date concisely. Admit you're working on doing a better job of staying in touch. If you've had some difficulties or challenges don't dwell on those. Look for ways to be a giver and reconnect.

Keep the conversation light and positive.

Bring good news or information to share. Read or listen to something interesting beforehand. Or simply read the day's news or an interesting article that gives you something to talk about. This could provide good fodder for conversation. Make sure it's a positive topic, and resist the urge to talk politics, religion, or other topics prone to controversy and high emotion.

Ask thoughtful questions to stimulate conversation.

When chatting ask "how" and "what" questions. Steer clear of "why" questions as they can seem harsh and nosy and can put people on the defensive. And also consider ditching the question, "What are you doing here?" This can sound stuffy and pretentious, as in, "I belong here but you don't."

Stick to safe and pleasant conversation topics.

Don't ask questions that are too personal or pry into private matters. Likewise don't divulge information about yourself or others that may be too personal or simply TMI (Too Much Information). Topics to avoid: health, diet, how much things cost, personal questions, gossip, vulgar jokes. In fact, avoid any gossip, complaining or negative conversation. This speaks more about you than whatever (or whoever) you are talking about. Plus it's just plain depressing and draining.

Be generous but sincere with compliments, and accept compliments graciously.

One woman I know strives to compliment every person she meets. She is always sincere and honest, and that makes her so lovable and attractive. If you are lucky enough to receive such a compliment, be gracious, smile, and simply say "Thank you." Don't deflect or make a big deal out of the comment, just accept it. Above all, don't fish for additional compliments.

Give others something to work with as you converse.

Don't just answer questions with simple yes and no answers. It's okay to elaborate a little and hold up your end of the exchange. In contrast, don't go overboard and ramble. A conversation partner with a glazed-over look is a signal you've gone on too long. Go for a 50:50 ratio of talking versus listening. When in doubt, listen more than you talk.

try this!

Utilize the power of conversation pieces. Comment on an interesting accessory the other person is wearing. Or wear a conversation-starter yourself, such as a piece of jewelry that was given to you by someone you love, was purchased somewhere interesting, or was handmade. (Again, never talk about how much an item costs.)

See someone you want to meet? Be bold, but brief and courteous.

If you see someone at an event you've always wanted to meet or someone you admire, it's okay to approach them politely and strike up a conversation. Be sure you're not interrupting another conversation when you approach. Tell the person something you admire or appreciate about them. If you knew he or she would be at the event beforehand, do some research so you have a connecting point. Keep it brief. Perhaps something like, "Excuse me, Ms. Jones? My name is Jenny Smith. You don't know me, but I am a fan of your work and

I just wanted you to know how much I enjoyed and benefited from your book." Chances are, if you are gracious and considerate, they'll really appreciate meeting you.

Feeling unsociable but still want to get out?

Try this approach. Choose to be in observation mode. There are days when you may not be in the right frame of mind to converse with new people. When you're feeling this way, why not attend an event with the primary intention of taking things slowly and simply observing? You might even discover that some of the most interesting people approach you because you've "turned it down a notch" and are more open and attractive to them, especially by those who aren't as high-energy or gregarious as you typically may be. You may actually be more open to receive in this state of mind. As an observer take note of the people who:

⁂ **Show up on time or even a little early.**

⁂ **Are appropriately and professionally dressed.**

⁂ **Show up prepared.**

⁂ **Exude radiant energy, friendliness, and warmth with everyone they meet.**

⁂ **Seem both genuine and confident.**

⁂ **Are alert, but at ease.**

⁂ **Are ready to engage in conversation.**

⁂ **Make a point to greet and receive greetings with a smile and eye contact.**

⁂ **Offer a firm but friendly handshake.**

⁂ **Are as interested in others as others are in them.**

If you don't have the chance to talk to these people at this event, make a note of who they are, and watch for them at the next gathering.

thoughtful next steps

If you have enjoyed meeting someone and see the possibility of continuing the conversation at some point in the future, there are several levels of next steps. The trick is to let the other person know of your interest without being too intrusive or demanding. Next steps might include agreeing to:

- ❋ **Exchange business cards and other collaterals.**

- ❋ **Add the person to your database and vice versa.**

- ❋ **Subscribe to each other's blogs or newsletters.**

- ❋ **Exchange social media information. (Facebook, Twitter, LinkedIn, etc.)**

- ❋ **Agree to schedule a follow-up phone conversation.**

- ❋ **Arrange to have coffee or lunch.**

- ❋ **Follow up in a few days or weeks or as otherwise advised.**

- ❋ **Be patient and stay in touch, but never cross the line into pestering or stalking.**

try this!

When you attend a networking event, you'll likely end up with business cards from people with whom you connected and want to build a relationship. Unfortunately, you may also end up with cards you didn't ask for, but were thrust at you by well-meaning networkers. It's time to note and sort.

First, as you go through the cards, write a note in the corner of each indicating the event at which you met them and the date. This will help you remember when and how you met, which is important information.

The A Pile. These are the cards from people with whom you clicked. You can see yourself staying in touch, possibly even doing business with them. As people and professionals they seem to align well with what you're about. You are ready to add them to your database and look forward to following up and getting to know them better.

The B Pile. These cards came from people you liked, but they didn't quite make the A grade. At least not yet. Maybe you didn't get to spend much time with them or they just didn't wow you. You will consider learning more about them, should you run into them again. They go in the B Pile. You may be going through these again. Hang on to them.

The C Pile. These cards came from people you don't have any sort of feeling about one way or another. You might have the opportunity to get to know them better and will do so if given the chance.

The Toss Pile. This may sound brutal, harsh, or crazy, but go ahead and do it: feel free to throw away any cards that came from people who just didn't resonate with you at all, were rude, brash, talked endlessly, or gave you the creeps. There is no reason to keep them and there is negative energy in these cards. You don't need them. In the circular file they go.

What to do with the ABC Piles: Add the A's to your database right away. Go through the B's and C's once or twice a year – once a quarter if you are building your database. If any of the cards/people graduate to A status as a result of further meetings, put them in your database. Similarly, be sure to go through, clean, and update your database once or twice a year.

Keep your promises and be consistent and considerate with your follow-up.

If in your exchanges with others you've made a promise to send along some information, make an introduction, or otherwise follow up, be sure to make good on your promise.

> For as much time and effort that people can put into networking, they often drop the ball here, hence the saying, "The fortune is in the follow-up." The fortune is there because so few actually follow up.

Find creative ways to give, share, and strengthen the relationship.

The spirit of giving helps keeps relationships alive and it doesn't have to be difficult, time consuming, or a quest that breaks your budget. It's simply a habit of considering and remembering others and helping them feel respected, valued, and good about themselves.

Keep learning and practicing.

Like any other skill, networking and connecting easily and successfully requires practice and continual learning and tweaking. Reread sections of this book. Choose a few areas to focus on, then move on to others. Find what works best for you. Keep adjusting your own networking formula and note where you feel confident and successful. Also note what just isn't a fit.

why do this work?

This is an easy one – the more you practice intentional, consistent, gracious networking, the more luck you'll have attracting and making solid connections with your people. As a result, your people will help you spread the word about you and your business.

CHAPTER **8**

*※ give first

THE ART OF MAKING QUALITY REFERRALS

In this chapter, you will:

- Learn how you can become a valuable, respected, and trusted referral resource.

- See how easy it is to base referral decisions on wise standards and policies.

- Discover who to refer and why, and who not to refer and why not.

- Read tips for making every referral or connection a win for all involved.

Kay had just joined a networking group and was attending a meeting for the first time. The people seated at each table were given two minutes each to give a brief self-introduction. They were also encouraged to mention one current need or challenge they faced in their businesses.

As each person introduced themselves and stated their needs, Kay was excited and blurted out instant recommendations to each person. "You've got to talk to my friend Bob. He does that." "Oh, Company XYZ can do that. You should call them." "I need to connect you with my neighbor, Julie. Here's her number. She really needs the work right now." The people at Kay's table began raising eyebrows and exchanging glances. Some were even hesitant to talk about themselves and their businesses for fear of being pounced upon by this over-eager woman.

After the meeting, Darline, one of Kay's tablemates and a seasoned and respected member of the group, gently pulled Kay aside. "We're so glad to have you with us today, Kay, but I can't help noticing that you seemed kind of wound-up. Were you a little nervous since this was your first meeting?"

Kay was taken aback. Nervous? Of course she wasn't nervous! She made it clear to Darline that she was proud of being an experienced networker, a go-getter, a giver, and a successful business woman. She had earned a wall full of awards for her top performance in her sales jobs and had a huge rolodex of contacts to match. Wasn't connecting and referring with enthusiasm and promptness the way to make an impression, make good contacts, and attract business?

"I'm sorry," Darline continued. "We love your energy and enthusiasm and know you mean well. It's just that we do things a little differently here. The power of this group is our focus on building deeper, stronger, long-term relationships. So when we listen to others and hear what they need, we give our recommendations a little more thought. We follow up, continue the conversation, ask more questions. Then we make our referrals and suggestions. I think you might earn more respect from the others in the group if you tried a less aggressive approach."

Maybe you know someone like Kay – a jazzed-up, highly caffeinated networker who connects with great eagerness and generosity, but also with wild abandon and even a little carelessness. People like Kay believe that's the way to demonstrate what successful connectors, referral sources, and givers they are. They have the best of intentions and are indeed givers – a good thing of course. But they can also be the bane of our networking existence, distracting us with misguided matchmaking attempts and carloads of referrals, connections, and introductions that bring us no true value and might even be the cause of some real headaches.

secrets of a true connector

Despite the story you just read about giving too much, too quickly and without much thought, it's still far better to be a giver in the networking world. When you give you not only demonstrate a spirit of generosity, abundance, and caring, you also have the potential to build trust and forge strong business relationships. But keep in mind you also have a huge responsibility to give purposefully and thoughtfully and with the intent of creating positive results for all. Your good reputation, your business, and your own ability to attract quality referrals depend on this.

Your goal is to become something far better and more valuable than another enthusiastic networker. You are choosing to become an *intentional* networker as well as a thoughtful connector and trusted resource. It's another step toward becoming the person everyone values and is glad they know. And the best part? Along the way you'll likely attract more quality referrals and opportunities yourself.

* * *

Be sure before you refer. Your reputation and your ability to attract referrals rely on it.

* * *

Every referral, recommendation, introduction, and connection creates a chain of events.

Anytime you initiate a connection, there is bound to be some kind of reaction. Your matchmaking efforts could be the best thing that ever happened to those involved, resulting in an ongoing ripple of goodwill, positive results, and appreciation. In contrast, a careless connection can set off waves of bewilderment, frustration, and drama, not to mention the loss of priceless time, resources, credibility, and goodwill.

With the former, you're the hero. With the latter, you're the goat. Which would you prefer?

Make every connection with care. Take the work of connecting seriously. Vow from this moment on to be thoughtful, discerning, and purposeful each time you make a referral, recommendation, introduction, and connection – or even an endorsement or testimonial. Believe that the time and resources that anyone involved in one of your connections will invest are as much yours as theirs. Care that much. After all, in the end your reputation will be affected for better or worse. And what's the value of a good reputation? Answer: priceless.

Think of it this way: if you were on a road trip without a map, got lost, and stopped to ask for directions, would you want the person you're asking to provide you with accurate information? Or would you want them to take a wild guess as to which way you should go? The latter would waste your time and fuel as well as exacerbate your frustrations. You certainly wouldn't reach your destination any faster. And what would you think of the person who gave you the careless directions?

It's time to start thinking like a true business matchmaker. You want to be someone who is known to provide quality and value in their recommendations, and is a success-minded, trustworthy business leader who carefully considers who or what would help others enjoy a positive outcome in any connecting situation.

slow down your referral reflex

It may sound counterintuitive, but the first step in making better connections is to *slow down.* Pause. Think. Ask questions. Review the options.

True, everything in the business world seems to move at the speed of light these days, competition is fierce, and he/she who hesitates can find themselves lost. What's more, being enthusiastic and helpful to others are positive traits. *However,* you'll find that most people, particularly the ones seeking stellar results, would rather receive fewer but higher quality, carefully considered referrals and introductions.

Listen to others' requests carefully, ask questions, and help them assess and clarify their needs. Sometimes the person who asks for a referral or recommendation hasn't had the opportunity to think through what they need. Don't try to be a psychic. Borrow techniques from the world of *consultative selling.* Help your colleague figure out what he or she needs by asking questions. Here are some examples:

- ❊ **Tell me more about what you're looking for.**

- ❊ **What are your expectations?**

- ❊ **What's most important to you?**

- ❊ **Do you have a budget in mind?**

- ❊ **Do you have a deadline or schedule?**

- ❊ **What/who have you tried in the past?**

- ❊ **What worked? What didn't?**

- ❊ **What end result would make it a home run?**

- ❊ **What would the ideal solution look like to you?**

The following story illustrates this point quite well. Alisha was at a networking luncheon and casually mentioned to the other women at the event that she really needed a part-time assistant. Before she had the chance to say anything else, such as what the job would entail, what skills she was seeking, what she could pay, and how many hours a week were required, all but one person in the conversation circle had whipped out pens and paper and had started scribbling down names and phone numbers of people they knew who were looking for work.

One woman in the circle, Connie, remained calm. She leaned over to Alisha and said quietly, "May I call you tomorrow? I'd like to ask you a few questions about what you need. I know of several resources that provide small businesses with sharp part-time assistants, virtual or onsite. I want to be clear on what you need this assistant to do for you to make sure these are the right resources for you."

As Alisha accepted the bits of paper with names and numbers from the others, she realized that Connie's approach was actually the most intriguing and promising. Wow, she thought, someone who is actually interested in helping me solve my challenge and isn't just interested in passing along names of their unemployed friends.

Connie and Alisha talked the next day. Connie was able to get more detail and clarity on what Alisha needed. The conversation also helped Alisha clarify her own thoughts. Alisha took down the phone number of a company Connie recommended and called them later that afternoon. They were responsive and said they could send a couple of resumes to Alisha right away.

Meanwhile, resumes began flooding into Alisha's email inbox and the phone started ringing with calls from the candidates the other people recommended. Unfortunately, most were seeking full-time jobs or weren't sure what they wanted. Some simply didn't have the right skills or experience Alisha needed. Some of them talked Alisha's ear off. Alisha found herself spending way too much time dealing with this flood of interest. All told, she spent two hours dealing with these responses.

In contrast, Alisha received the two resumes from Connie's recommended resource. Both candidates seemed like excellent fits for Alisha's needs. She eventually hired one of them to help her get through the projects that had kept her up nights. She plans to use the service again the next time she has the need for some extra help.

And Connie has earned a spot on Alisha's list of most valued contacts, simply because Connie took the time to ask questions, listen closely, understand what Alisha needed, and was thoughtful in recommending a resource that could produce a good result.

> The quality of your referrals and those you refer creates a tangible extension of your reputation and brand. What do you want this brand to be? Quick and random? Or thoughtful and results-oriented?

Another way to hit the pause button is to ask if you can give any request "The Overnight Test." I appreciate it when I'm explaining my vision, goals, challenges, and needs to someone and they say, "Hmm. I may have a couple of options for you, but let me think on it just to be sure which one might be the best fit." Wow! What a refreshing difference it can make when the other person means it and follows through, sharing a spot-on referral or connection the next morning. Some of the most valuable and long-time contacts and resources in my database came to me this way. And it seems the more urgent, important, and potentially critical or expensive the need, the greater the need for recommendations to be well thought out.

be particular: develop referral standards, policies, and criteria

Earlier we covered how to develop and abide by your custom-created standards, policies, and criteria. You can apply similar techniques with how you make referrals and connections by instituting policies, standards, and criteria that will guide you. For example, ask yourself:

What traits or credentials must people or organizations have before you trust them, are willing to bet your reputation on them, and feel confident referring them? How long and how well must you know them? Are you willing to recommend or refer someone even if you've never worked with them yourself?

> You don't make friends, earn trust, serve as a positive
> influence, or build a sterling reputation by making
> haphazard recommendations. You do so by being
> thoughtful and discerning. Creating more noise and
> distractions and wasting others' time or money won't do it.

try this!

Create a list of those you know you can refer with confidence – your Referral List. Once you are clear on your standards, policies, and criteria, use them to guide you as you create your Referral List. This is an exclusive and ever-evolving short list of people and organizations in various professions and categories that you believe you can refer with the utmost confidence. You know and trust these people and organizations. Maybe you've even worked with them or hired them yourself. You are certain they will do a great job and reflect well on you when you refer or connect them. You are willing to bet your reputation on them. They are a positive extension of your brand. They reinforce your high standards. More on this in a bit.

tips for making better referrals

Offer several options or choices whenever possible.

Even if you're completely confident in the people, organizations, or resources you refer, no two situations are the same and no two people will have exactly the same tastes, preferences, or opinions. That's why offering your colleagues several referral options is a valuable bonus. Be sure to share your insights about each choice. After that it's up to your colleagues to decide on the best options.

> As you make referrals to others consider this: what if you had to offer a "money-back guarantee" on anyone or anything you refer? In a way you do, except that your reputation is priceless.

Add caveats or disclaimers when necessary.

Let's say you've had terrific luck with the company that prints your business cards. They've given you great pricing, have done a terrific job on your projects over the years, and consistently offer fast turnaround. Yet they have some limitations on the kinds of printing they can do. For example, you've only had them do basic two-color printing. Perhaps the print shop isn't exactly the picture of neatness and cleanliness and it's located in a not-so-great part of town. The employees are nice and good at what they do, but their tattoos and long hair can make them look a little intimidating. Be sure to share this and any other pertinent information so your colleagues aren't surprised.

Here's another example: say you're referring someone you've only recently met. (This can be risky, by the way.) You were initially impressed, but you don't really *know* them, haven't *actually* worked with them, or even heard anything about them one way or another. This means you can't be certain of their capabilities. Be sure to share this in the referral process. Encourage the party to whom you're making the referral to use an extra dose of due diligence to decide if the match is a good one for them. In other words, buyer beware.

Consider whether you're even the right person to make the referral.

Cal sells office equipment. His clients are CPAs, attorneys, doctors, therapists, and small businesses. When one of Cal's customers mentioned he needed a copywriter for some ads and marketing materials, Cal reacted. He recommended the first writer he thought of, his neighbor Sheila. Sheila is indeed a freelance writer looking for work. You may be thinking, "How nice. Cal's helping out his neighbor." Not so fast. This referral could be a problem. What Cal doesn't know is that Sheila specializes in writing manuals, white papers, and product specification sheets for high-tech and scientific instrumentation firms. She has no experience with promotional copywriting. Cal doesn't understand that recommending a technical writer for a copywriting project is akin to recommending hiking boots as the proper footwear for a formal cocktail party. And because Sheila is chomping at the bit to bring in some work, any work at all, she may convince Cal's customer that she can do the work.

Could this referral work out? Possibly. Some writers can adapt very easily to different needs. Would it have been better to recommend the kind of writer who has the copywriting experience needed? Probably. But since Cal's specialty is office equipment, he may not be the best person to make the referral in the first place. Cal should have passed on this request or brought in a colleague who knows some good copywriters.

The lesson here: before you offer up a referral, recommendation, or connection, be sure you understand what exactly is being requested and make sure you have a solid and appropriate recommendation to offer. If not, be truthful and steer the person to a better resource if you know of one. Or simply say, "I'm sorry, I'm not the right person to ask."

Don't refer people to others simply because:

* **They are your relatives, friends, colleagues, neighbors, or acquaintances.**
* **You met them at the last networking event you attended.**
* **You have their business card on file.**
* **You follow them on social media or read their blog.**
* **They have a lot of followers on social media.**
* **You belong to the same club or organization.**

- ❋ They asked for your referrals (but haven't earned your trust or endorsement yet).

- ❋ They have slick, attractive marketing materials.

- ❋ There is a lot of hype about them in the media.

- ❋ They have seemingly impressive credentials.

- ❋ They are facing hard times and need a "break."

> If you're like many people, your personal and business relationships may sometimes merge. Both are important, but be sure strong personal feelings or close relationships don't muddle your judgment about how they fit into your business – or someone else's.

Don't put people on the spot.

When making a referral, recommendation, introduction, or connection make sure it has the potential to benefit *all* involved. For example, if you recommend that Colleague A seek a favor or freebie from Colleague B, you may be helping Colleague A, but you're really putting Colleague B on the spot. This can create not only awkwardness, but potential resentment. Who are you to suggest Colleague B give away her time and expertise? Don't do this to your valued friends and colleagues.

In contrast, if you refer Colleague A to Colleague B for some paid consulting, they decide to work together, and the relationship creates good results, you'll look great for matching them up. You all win. Further, if the project Colleague A and Colleague B worked on together has a beneficial ripple effect on others, all the better.

Imagine how amazing it would feel (and what it would do for your reputation) if most of your referrals and connections created an avalanche of positive results for all involved.

* * *

what a not-so-great referral resource looks like

Consider my colleague Adele. Adele wants very badly, maybe even desperately, to win a place in my rolodex as a valued peer and referral resource. She tries repeatedly to win my favor by sending so-called leads my way. God bless her, she tries to be helpful, but nearly always misses the mark.

For example, one day she called to tell me about her Uncle Joe. He was thinking about writing a book and needed a ghostwriter. Adele was hoping this would be a good opportunity for one of the writers in my talent network. I asked her some routine questions about Uncle Joe as well as his needs, budget, and timeline. Adele was a little uncertain, even a bit evasive. Finally, she admitted that Uncle Joe was actually a rather cantankerous old coot who could be very eccentric, demanding, and difficult. On top of that he was a cheapskate.

"Adele," I implored, "why would anyone in my network want to work with this man?" Where was the win? For anyone? Adele quickly saw the problem and sheepishly apologized for taking up my time. Crisis averted.

Unfortunately for Adele, this latest attempt at throwing me a bone backfired and has made me question the value of anything she will send my way in the future.

what a reliable referral resource looks like

Here's an example of what making consistently good referrals and recommendations can do for your reputation, business, and career. My colleague Renée Trudeau is a successful coach, published author, and professional speaker and workshop facilitator. She is becoming widely known for the work she does with women seeking balance in their lives and work. It's no secret she is purposeful and particular in all she does, from the ways she spends her time to the exquisite layout of her first book, *The Mother's Guide to Self Renewal: How to Reclaim, Rejuvenate, and Re-Balance Your Life.*

When Renée sends something or someone my way, I generally pay keen attention. Among the referrals Renée has sent me is a woman who is now a valued colleague and close friend, Sara Canaday. Sara is a leadership consultant, professional speaker, and personal brand strategist. Renée's initial referral came by email with a description of who Sara was, how Renée knew her, what she knew about Sara, and why she felt she was someone I needed to know. Knowing Renée had thought this referral through carefully and had taken the time to understand my business and needs, I immediately set up a coffee date with Sara. I found her to be not only brilliant and delightful, but someone with whom I wanted to do business. That was more than eight years ago. Sara has made a tremendous difference in my life and business. I give Renée credit for matching us up. What a gift!

Start your Referral List.

To get your Referral List started, and to set the benchmarks by which all those you consider for your List will be measured, go through your database and choose the five people or organizations you feel absolutely comfortable and confident referring to others. You are willing, here and now, to bet your reputation on them. You trust them implicitly to do a good job. You know through first-hand experience that they do excellent work consistently and offer flawless customers service. You know they have a stellar reputation that goes back years. You know they won't let you down. And if anything goes wrong, they will make things right. This is your benchmark of excellence.

Who are these people or companies? Now list the traits that make you like and trust them.

Next, think about this: who are your top five referral resources? These are the five go-to people in your database who have over the years provided you with referrals, connections, introductions, and resources that have been consistently helpful, stellar, and spot on. Make another list for these people, noting the traits that make them special.

Finally, compare your lists. What traits do the people on both lists share? See any patterns or parallels?

How to evaluate your Referral List prospects:

❉ **Know the must-have traits for anyone on your List.**

❉ **Have one-on-one visits over coffee or lunch.**

❉ **Know it can take several of these visits to get to know them. Don't rush it.**

❉ **"Interview" them informally (they don't have to know it – just ask revealing questions).**

❉ **Get to know them as people, not just as professionals.**

❉ **Learn their standards and beliefs – and note if they walk their talk.**

❉ **Observe and note how they deal with others.**

❋ Listen to what others say about them and what you hear via the grapevine.

❋ Google them. What's in their background?

❋ Learn their niche, strengths, pricing, and style.

❋ Do business with them yourself – try them out.

❋ If you know each other virtually or via social media:

  • schedule phone chats.

  • compare notes on when or whether you will be in the same city or at the same business event.

  • read each other's blogs and other materials.

* * *

Anyone and anything you refer or recommend is a reflection on you, your brand, your business, your reputation.

* * *

more referral tips

Respect, adhere to, and uphold your policies and standards.

Don't give in to impulse, high-pressure referral tactics, or even those cocktails you've indulged in when you are about to refer business. Stay true to your own standards, and be aware that not everyone will have standards as particular as yours or have the same tastes and experience you have.

Allow your Referral List to grow and evolve over time.

You'll gradually add more people and organizations to the list as they win your trust. You may also take people off your list if they let you down, move away, change careers, or their reputation tarnishes. Your standards will continue to become more refined and sophisticated over time and with practice. You will become more particular. That's the whole point. When others know you have high standards and expectations that you uphold and use discernment as you make referrals and recommendations, they will trust you and be attracted to you as a resource. They know they can count on you for good information and will likely do business with you as well. That's influence and an excellent and hard-won source of power.

Keep your Referral List private.

As you build your Referral List, you'll begin to see it for the incredibly valuable asset it is. Keep your list private and don't post it or randomly share it in its entirety with others. You've put time, thought, and research into it. Use it as a "power tool." Furthermore, no one needs to know whether they've made your Referral List or not. And don't add someone to your list just because they've asked for your referrals. Anyone you refer business to should earn that privilege.

Become a fan and advocate.

Unless you choose to keep them a secret (and maybe that's the case) letting others know about your best colleagues and the positive experiences you have with their businesses is valuable. Offer to connect them – mindfully, of course. Introduce them to someone you believe they should know. But again, be sure it is likely to create a win-win, not just noise or even awkwardness.

If it's a fit, spotlight your best people in your articles, books, blog posts, or tweets. Ask them for their comments and reviews if it's appropriate. Yes, you are technically asking them for something here, but you are also honoring them by showing you trust them to provide a good contribution. You are also offering them an opportunity to be heard by your audience. It's free publicity, an endorsement, and productive cross-marketing. Perhaps they will ask you to do the same for them. You can also comment on, and review their books or articles – you don't need an invitation to do this for your best connections, and it can be very helpful to them.

> Show generous and ongoing appreciation to anyone with whom you have a strong, positive, and mutually beneficial referral or connections relationship. These are some of the most valuable people and organizations in your network. Respect them and their time.

Approach every connection with grace and thoughtfulness.

For example, if you believe Mary should meet Deborah, you could copy them both on an email where you make a virtual introduction. These are the steps to follow:

- ❉ **Let them know that you'd like to make the introduction.**

- ❉ **Offer some basic information about each person.**

- ❉ **Say why you believe they should know each other, and how they'd both benefit.**

- ❉ **Humbly ask them to consider the connection.**

- ❉ **If they believe it's worth their time, suggest they take next steps – a phone conversation, a coffee meeting, etc. No pressure. Ever.**

- ❉ **Thank them for their time and consideration.**

- ❉ **Encourage them to offer honest feedback.**

Realize that perfection is impossible.

Even when you are extremely particular and mindful with your referrals and connections, expecting 100% perfection is unrealistic. There will be times when a referral or connection just doesn't work out for any number of reasons beyond human control. It's going to happen. People are human and imperfect. Chemistry and many other impossible-to-harness factors are at work. Instead of expecting perfection as you make referrals and connections, strive for consistent excellence. You will significantly increase your odds of being a noteworthy catalyst for good results.

Encourage any parties you are referring to own up to their responsibilities.

While it's critical to make the best connections you possibly can, the people to whom you make connections have a responsibility to make good judgments as well. Graciously let everyone involved know that your opinions and judgments should never be seen as a substitute for their own. Final decisions are their responsibility.

Avoid the scourge of triangulation.

This occurs when three parties are involved in a situation, referral, or relationship and two of the three get together to discuss, gripe about, or even bad-mouth the third. Typically it's Person 3 who needs to hear what Persons 1 and 2 are discussing in order to fix the problem or make any improvements. Usually Persons 1 and 2 are afraid to engage in such a frank discussion. We've all been guilty of this and it rarely, if ever, makes a situation better. In fact, it often perpetuates or worsens the problem.

> In referral situations where you're not sure you can create good results, it's usually better to back away than to take the risk. When it doubt, stay out.

Referral red flags: watch out for these potential hazards:

- ☀ **Professional organizations or leads groups that strongly suggest you do business with or make referrals to other members, purely because they are members.**

- ☀ **People who approach you and aggressively ask for your business, leads, or referrals before you've had ample time to get to know them and their work.**

- ☀ **People who pressure you into exclusive referral agreements and promise to give you referrals in exchange for getting yours.**

a few words about referral fees

Before writing this book I spent more than twenty years making and receiving referrals. I currently have referral fee arrangements with the people who are members of my exclusive referral network. I have a letter of agreement that explains my terms up front before any referrals are made, which is the best way to do it. Having the terms in writing keeps us literally on the same page and helps us quickly settle any what-if or what-now situations as they come up.

If an opportunity arises that is a fit for someone who is not currently in my referral network, I discuss my fees with them before making the connection. Discussing fees after connections are made generally leads to ill feelings. I had a colleague who referred a client to me many years ago, and then three months into the deal asked me for a percentage of the business. I was shocked. Had she brought this up at the time of the referral I would have considered the arrangement, but to bring it up that late in the game was just plain odd, if not offensive. An always upfront, no-surprises policy about any referral fees is by far the best route to take. My standard referral fee is 15%, although I adjust it under special circumstances.

Occasionally I make referrals and introductions purely because it's the right thing to do and the best fit for all involved. In those cases, I'm not seeking a monetary return. In some cases a referral fee may not be allowed by law or the ethical standards of the profession. Many of these situations are more about building goodwill and reinforcing my reputation as a capable, trustworthy business matchmaker focused on quality relationships and results.

I have one such relationship where I frequently send customers to a colleague without asking for or collecting any referral fees. We came to this agreement after many years of doing business together. We realized there was a special quality in the way our respective businesses complemented each other and the balance and reciprocity of our referrals. Those qualities transcended any exchange of currency. We stay in a near-perfect state of symbiotic balance and are happy with the relationship just the way it is. I'd do something for her gratis and she graciously reciprocates with business advice, tips, priceless opportunities, discounted services, as well as testimonials and recommendations. We have bolstered each other's businesses and reputations in ways that cannot be measured in dollars. Many business relationships are like this.

follow up, gather, and leverage feedback

There is a critical step that even the most seasoned connectors sometimes forget: leveraging constructive feedback. It's doubling back, requesting honest reactions, opinions, and other information. It's making sure you made a good referral or connection that created value for all. It's learning what you might have done differently or better. The information you gain in this phase will help you fine tune your referral list and referral skills immensely. Yes, it will require some extra time and effort, but you'll find it is well worth it.

Ask for honest feedback at various stages of the referral process. For example, if you were to recommend a graphic designer (or several candidates) to a colleague in need of a logo and visual branding help, you can simply ask, "How are things going?" or "How did things go?" at the various stages, including:

- **During the initial screening and interviewing process**
- **At the bidding or estimating stage**
- **After any initial working stages**
- **When the work is finished**
- **If and when additional work is done**

Types of feedback you can gather include:

- **First impressions**
- **Responsiveness**
- **Attitude**
- **Professionalism**
- **Talent**
- **Service**
- **Effectiveness**
- **Attention to detail**

- ❈ **Problem-solving abilities**

- ❈ **Pricing/value**

- ❈ **Quality**

- ❈ **What went well**

- ❈ **What could they have done better**

- ❈ **Other "need-to-know" feedback**

What to do with feedback you receive:

- ❈ **Share it tactfully with the person or organization you referred so they can learn where they excelled and where they can improve.**

- ❈ **Show gratitude and appreciation to those who took great care with your referral and made you look good.**

- ❈ **Learn from it in a way that helps you connect and make referrals more thoughtfully.**

- ❈ **Add it as a notation to your referral database.**

- ❈ **Use it to create a ranking system for your good, better, and best people and organizations to refer.**

referral forensics

Given that sometimes referrals go awry, what should you do when a referral or introduction goes badly? Reflect on what happened, and ask yourself some questions, such as:

- ❈ **What was the request?**

- ❈ **Who or what was referred?**

- ❈ **What happened along the way?**

- ❊ **What was the result?**

- ❊ **What factors were at work?**

- ❊ **How did it benefit or hurt you and the others involved?**

- ❊ **What is your attitude about those involved?**

- ❊ **What does how the situation was handled say about the parties involved?**

- ❊ **What will you do differently next time?**

- ❊ **How can you make good on what went wrong?**

yellow flag referrals: blunders to avoid

There are many situations that, by their very nature, are the breeding ground for impulsive, poor quality, or other potentially negative referrals and connections. Watch for these Yellow Flag Referrals – both giving them and being the recipient (or victim) of them.

The Hit-and-Run Introduction.

Ever receive an email from a colleague that gives you the name and contact information of someone they think you should know and vice versa – and that's it? No further explanation, as if you're supposed to guess what they were thinking? "Dear Sally, I ran into my colleague John Adams the other day and realized you two need to know each other. I've copied John here. Hoping you two can set up a time to meet. Enjoy! Sincerely, Steve." Likely there is a good reason why your colleague had the urge to connect you, but wouldn't it be nice to know what it is?

The Happy Hour Referral.

You met a new contact over cocktails and really hit it off. You have instantly become best business buddies and are ready to refer each other for all kinds of business situations. You've bonded. Okay, so the fact that there was alcohol involved might be your first clue that, as in dating, there is a chance your judgment has been impaired. It might behoove you to find out if you still feel the same giddy enthusiasm about this person when morning comes and you are completely sober. So rather than making a spontaneous and possibly unfortunate referral that might forever tarnish your otherwise spotless reputation, go forward cautiously over coffee or lunch. Get to know each other further. Ask around. Check references. Google. Let the relationship develop before you refer them to anyone (or accept their referrals). It just makes sense, don't you think?

The Sympathy Referral.

You have a friend, acquaintance, or colleague who has fallen on hard times – divorce, bankruptcy, illness, layoff, financial woes, etc. It's a good and compassionate thing to offer support and advice when someone is hurting or in need. But don't pawn them off on others *simply* because they are having difficulties. *Needing* is not the same as *deserving*. If you would not feel confident referring them under the *best* of circumstances, the only way you should do so now is with an honest disclaimer about their true abilities (or lack thereof) or at least a sincere and true statement of how little you actually know about them or the quality of their work. Some people actually rise to the occasion when they are facing adversity; others bring a whirl-wind of drama and disaster with them wherever they go.

The Impulsive Referral.

You blurt out the first name or idea that comes to mind when someone tells you what they are seeking. The only way this one works is if you are: a) quick, but seasoned in the business of making referrals and picky as all get-out, b) a walking database of all *the* best people and resources in town, and c) have an almost freakish and psychic knack for successful connecting. Still, it pays to ask for more details on what your friend or colleague needs before giving them any specific recommendations.

The Quid Pro Quo Referral.

This one seems to be emblazoned into the psyche of the business world. And not following it almost seems counterintuitive, if not shocking and a reason to be tarred and feathered publicly. As you might guess, the common belief is that if I refer business to you, you should automatically and without hesitation refer business back to me. I don't know about you, but I've received some lovely referrals from some people to whom I will be forever grateful. But honestly, there is little if any chance I could in good faith reciprocate. Why? They just aren't that good at what they do. Generosity and gonzo networking skills are not necessarily signs of competence and professionalism. If you don't feel comfortable sending referrals back to someone, you might consider rewarding them in another way. A nice gift card. Some free advice. Flowers. A one-way trip to an exotic locale. Surely you can come up with creative – and safe – ways to return the favor and express genuine gratitude.

The Proximity Referral.

Do not refer (or expect referrals from) someone *merely* because they live or work near you or go the same meetings, social events, church, tennis club, yoga class, coffee shop, or dog park. These are great places to make new contacts and find new resources, but use the same filters here you would use anywhere else.

The Brother-in-Law Referral.

Likewise, do not refer (or expect referrals from) someone *merely* because they are in some way related to you, either by blood or by law. In fact, be doubly cautious here. Remember, if things go badly, your relative will still be your relative.

The Hobbyist-Dabbler Referral.

Yes, I confess I am handy with the electric clippers when it comes to giving my son the basic #3 buzz cut he currently desires. I've even given him a snappy Mohawk for that championship soccer match. But I would never in a million years expect you to recommend me to someone who needs a good hair stylist. Likewise, just because someone knows a little bit about this or that, has taken a class or workshop, or does a certain activity in their spare time, it doesn't necessarily mean they are an expert worthy of a professional referral.

The Informational Interview Referral.

I'm not a fan of the informational interview (a.k.a. a meeting in which one person is basically asking for free information or advice from another more experienced, successful, or connected person). The only way I see it as a win-win is if *both* parties are *completely* agreeable to taking the time to do them and follow mutually agreeable guidelines. Also, the interviewer (the underling asking the questions) should take the time to know his or her purpose for the meeting, prepare good questions, be efficient in asking them, be über respectful of the interviewee's time, and be willing to return the favor several times over. They can at least pick up the tab if they are meeting at a restaurant (preferably a nice one) over lunch. So do your colleagues a favor and be sure to ask them how they feel about informational interviews before you ever recommend them to participate in one.

The Brain-Picking Referral.

Like the referral above, unless you are sure the recipient of this referral is totally okay with offering free advice or meeting over coffee for some Q & A, don't send them along. If you are often the target of relentless brain-picking match-ups, you may want to come up with some Rules of Engagement or policies that the brain-picker must follow. I have developed several such policies and they are posted clearly on my bulletin board by my desk to help me deflect (or at least manage) these time-wasters graciously and efficiently.

The What-the-Heck Referral.

This is connecting that has gone terribly awry. Basically, it's the referral or request that you did not ask for and cannot make any sense of whatsoever. The spam that lands in your inbox because someone gave out or acquired your email address or randomly passed along your business card. The phone call or introduction that puts you on the spot and makes you uncomfortable. The person who asks for a meeting or your business; solicits a recommendation or endorsement on LinkedIn or Facebook; wants your random vote for an award; or sends you a demo tape, manuscript, portfolio, life story, or an audacious request for a favor. And the kicker is, you've never met them before in your *entire life*. The kind of referral that makes you want to say, "What the …?" Hence the name.

The False Endorsement Referral.

This one fries me. This is when you generously pass along some information to someone about a job or an opportunity and the person inaccurately exaggerates their relationship with you or tells others that you "recommended them." I mean, honestly. Have they no shame? The proper way to do this is to say "I received this information from …" This implies generosity, not familiarity or endorsement.

The BFF Referral.

This is where you've met someone once or twice at networking events and suddenly word is that they're dropping your name left and right, referring to you as "a really close friend." Please. That just smacks of desperation.

The Hot Potato Referral.

This is the referral that lands in your lap, along with clear signs that it has already been passed along repeatedly – and rather decisively. Quite possibly for good reason. If ever there was a clear signal that this might be a Client from Hell, this is it. Maybe not. But be cautious nonetheless. And on another note, please don't pass a Hot Potato Referral along to anyone you care about, respect, or need in your world. They will not appreciate being put on the spot or being sucked into the hellish vortex of Hot Potato-ness. At all.

frequently asked questions about referrals

What should I do if I make a referral and it just doesn't work out? Should I apologize?

Absolutely. Furthermore, take the time to find out what went wrong so you can adjust your Referral List accordingly. Sometimes one party or the other didn't hold up their end of the deal or had unreasonable expectations; sometimes it's just bad chemistry or bad luck. Either way, the more information you can gather the less likely you are to repeat the mistake.

What should I do if word on the street about someone I refer a lot isn't that good?

If a person's or company's reputation is tarnished, find out specifics. Sometimes you'll discover it's a rumor. People can be mean and make things up. Yet other times you'll find it's the truth. Reputations are delicate and contagious. Protecting yours is your #1 job.

What if someone I meet at a networking event asks me flat out for referrals: how can I graciously let them know that I have to be cautious about who I refer business to?

Tell them you have strict policies about whom you give your referrals to and that you'll need to learn more about them before you can even consider such an arrangement.

why do this work?

Giving better referrals and making better connections helps you build your credibility and reputation. You show that you care about quality, respect others' time and resources, and demonstrate that you have good judgment and discerning taste. You know what you're doing, and you become a respected go-to resource and business person. You build your brand, and your credibility and stock goes way up. People trust you, and you develop a powerful and highly valued referral network – which you can tap into yourself.

Knowing how to give and follow up on high-quality referrals and connections helps you *attract* better referrals. This, in turn, builds your business, and allows you to do what you do best. Everyone wins.

CHAPTER 9

✳ reap your reward

ATTRACTING QUALITY REFERRALS

In this chapter, you will:

- Learn that quality referrals up your chances of closing business deals – by a lot.

- Read about ways to let people know what kind of business you want, and what you don't.

- Understand that receiving quality referrals is based on trust – and hard work.

Korey owns a photography studio that specializes in headshots and portraits. Over the years she's done excellent work, has run efficient and successful businesses, and has been a consistent and strategic networker. She no longer attends every event, but focuses on the ones that are a fit for her and are attended by people in the markets she serves. Korey knows her brand and who her clients and potential clients are and focuses on meeting and serving them enthusiastically. Her tagline "Photographer Standing By" sends the message that she is ready to serve you, when you are ready. Yet you will never see or hear Korey shamelessly peddling or pushing her services on anyone.

In addition, Korey makes scheduling easy, and offers pricing that is affordable, even to small businesses and solopreneurs. She also works to see that the experience of getting your portrait taken is fun, easy, and stress-free. She understands the insecurities and discomfort many people experience with having their photo taken.

Korey offers excellent recommendations on what to wear, is creative in her sets, uses both natural and studio lighting, and can touch up your makeup or hair in a pinch. Finally, she makes the process of selecting your favorite shots easy, is a master at touching up your photos so you look your absolute best (but still like you), and offers easy payment options. You walk out of Korey's studio with photos and a CD in hand – and a smile on your face.

Korey also guarantees her work. If you decide you're not satisfied with your photos, she will retake them. If you ever have a request that's not her specialty, she respectfully declines and works with you to find a reliable referral or resource.

If all this isn't enough, Korey participates regularly in philanthropic and community projects, hosts events so her clients can meet, mix and mingle, and generously (but judiciously) offers referrals to other businesses, if she believes in the quality of their work or product.

In short, Korey runs a consistently good, customer-focused business that brings value to her fellow entrepreneurs. She knows her strengths, brand, and market, and she focuses on serving it professionally to the best of her ability. She is someone you feel comfortable referring and has earned that privilege because of how she conducts herself and her business and how she treats her clients.

Is it any wonder that Korey's business is booming? She has done and continues to do what it takes to make herself irresistibly referable.

referrals are a privilege you earn, not a right you simply ask for

I wish I had a dime for every business person who approached me asking for my referrals or tips on how they could attract more referrals for their business. It seems everyone wants to know the secrets of attracting more business, more clients, more good contacts, more opportunities, and more good information via referrals. They know it's the single best route to growing a business, thriving in challenging times, reducing marketing expenses, shortening and streamlining sales cycles, attracting ideal customers, and building profitable businesses.

One study out of the Small Business Administration reveals that your chance of closing the deal on a referral is around sixty percent. In contrast, your chance of adding new clients via cold calls drops to a mere ten percent. No wonder everyone dreads making cold calls. The activity comes with a ninety percent failure rate!

Given this data you'd think that business people would do whatever it takes to understand how to become more referable. Yet that's not always the case. Many people believe there is a quick, once-and-done solution. A magic bullet. Build a better website. Find more followers on Facebook or Twitter. Attend more networking events. Hand out more business cards. Go out to lunch or coffee more. Send out more promotions. It's not that simple.

In addition, some people behave as if all they have to do is ask – that they have a right to ask others for referrals. After all, the ancient wisdom is, "Ask and you shall receive."

Again, it's not as easy as that.

Creating referrals happens when you build a great business, offer noteworthy service or an amazing product, exude a strong, authentic, attractive, and reliable brand and reputation as a person, and consistently invest in strategic networking and building high-quality relationships. There is no one step that will make it happen for your business. You've got to do the work and invest in the steps and strategies it takes to earn referrals. That's why this chapter comes at the end, rather than at the beginning, of this book.

> If there is one secret in this book here it is: if you've read the
> previous chapters and act strategically on the information,
> you are well on your way to attracting the respect, relation-
> ships, and referrals you so desire for your business. It's as
> easy and as challenging as that.

Because you want to attract rewarding relationships, referrals, and results for your business, let's do a quick review of the concepts mapped out in the previous chapters of this book.

Know and be clear on who you are, what your purpose is, and what you believe in.

If others don't understand, feel, or "get" who you really are and what you stand for after meeting, talking, and spending time with you, it will be difficult for them to know or remember you. They also may not understand how to suggest helpful resources, opportunities, or referrals to you. Furthermore, when people don't feel they know you, they also may not be ready to trust you. And without trust, there is no future for the relationship.

Know what you want: have a vision, set intentions, and establish goals.

If others don't know or understand what you're seeking or trying to accomplish, and how they may be able to help you, they can't choose to send opportunities your way. The person who replied, "Oh pretty much anything" when asked what kind of work she was looking for was an excellent example of this. How vague, unmemorable, and "all over the place" can you get?

Build and exude an attractive, authentic, consistent personal brand.

This isn't just something you show the world via your logo, business cards, brochures, or website. Your brand also includes your daily behaviors, beliefs, and practices; what you say, do, post on Twitter or Facebook; and otherwise demonstrate and reinforce every day. It's about how you show up; how you dress, and choose to present and "package" yourself; and how you speak to and treat others. If people don't experience a positive first impression from you, see a consistent continuation of that first impression, and believe you walk your talk as they are getting to know you, they won't remember you, trust you, or see you as someone they value and choose to help. You cannot build credibility without a positive first impression followed convincingly by the brand and everyday. Cohesive actions that back it up.

Focus on quality in your connections and associations and discover who your people are.

There is no good reason to have hundreds of shallow, meaningless, frustrating, or even destructive connections and relationships. There is every reason to build a thoughtful, strategic portfolio of people who bring value to you and appreciate you and vice versa. Go through your database, do the 80:20 math, and identify the twenty percent who have made a difference to you and your business. Focus on them. Analyze why they add value to you and your business. Further analyze how and where you met them. This is your benchmark for attracting more quality in your connections.

Graciously say no and set limits and boundaries regarding anything that doesn't work for you and your business.

Focus on what's best for you and your business, set some policies and guidelines, and then work up the gumption and discipline to say a firm but gracious "no thank you" to anything and anyone pulling at your time, attention, energy, or resources. You'll have more time for what you want and value, including serving your best clients and attracting more valuable connections.

Build and cultivate strong, lasting business relationships with your people.

Focus on building and staying connected to solid, lasting, win-win relationships with your best clients, friends, and colleagues. It takes energy to keep these good relationships going, but it's well worth it. By weeding out what doesn't work for you, you have more to invest in what does.

Know how to attract and initiate quality relationships in group settings.

It's necessary to get out into the world in person, to meet and spend face-to-face time with people. But this isn't about glad-handing and pitching business cards to everyone in the room. This is about showing up, strategically and regularly, creating good first impressions consistently, having a positive attitude, and making others feel comfortable around you. Once you do all that, it's your job to spot and focus on your people. Being out and about is your time to bolster your existing relationships and make new connections with those who have potential.

Send quality referrals, connections, and recommendations to others.

When you take the time, and make the effort to be thoughtful in how you make introductions, referrals, and recommendations, you will most likely create positive results for everyone involved, rather than just stirring up the sand. People, particularly those who are very busy, selective, and successful, will remember and appreciate your thoughtful generosity. You will further build your reputation and brand as someone who is selective, but also trustworthy, generous, and interested in helping and advancing others. This is the kind of "paying it forward" that will eventually come back around to you in spades.

referrals are about respect and trust

When it comes to referrals and recommendations, it's so easy to become ambitious, goal-oriented, and overly focused on making a sale or nabbing a new client. This is when drive, enthusiasm, and the desire to win can unfortunately lead to the repelling traits of impatience, rudeness, and aggressiveness. So the numero uno rule here is: never ask for referrals until you've established a relationship.

> It's one thing to share information on what you do, whom you
> serve, and what makes you unique and valuable. It's quite
> another to blatantly ask for referrals, leads, connections, and
> introductions or to assume others will "spread the word" on
> your behalf.

Do you want to be viewed as a presumptuous peddler or as a respected professional interested in mutually beneficial relationships and results? With this in mind, asking for someone's business, for referrals, or for them to promote your business, product, or service before you've proven yourself and established a relationship can easily backfire on you.

A recent experience comes to mind that illustrates this point. My husband and I were dining at a restaurant one evening and were experiencing one frustration and snafu after another. The waiter kept trying to describe and push items we did not want, the service was slow and clumsy, the kitchen was out of some of our favorite menu items, and what we finally ordered was prepared incorrectly and served with hilariously poor timing. The waiter and kitchen staff made several additional mistakes that affected not only the quality of the food, but our overall dining experience.

In addition, when the disinterested, disingenuous manager finally deduced there were issues, his attempt at "making good" (and I use that term loosely) was truly lame and unimpressive. I wanted to blurt out, "No, I'd rather not stay for dessert when I've just had the worst dining experience of the decade!" We were fuming by that time and could hardly wait to pay the tab and make our exit.

The evening went from awful to ridiculous when the waiter finally trotted over to our table to present us with the bill (which had not been modified nor discounted) and said enthusiastically, "Hey, thanks for dining with us, folks. Come on back and see us again soon – and be sure to tell your friends about us!"

My husband and I exchanged wide-eyed glances and communicated with each other in that special silent language only long-married couples share, "Did we just hear that?"

As you can imagine, we've not been back to that restaurant nor have we recommended it to our friends.

> Take a step back from yourself and your business. Ask
> yourself if you are doing everything you can to take good
> care of the customers and connections you value and
> become the referral magnet you want to be. After all,
> when someone sends you a referral, it's not only an act
> of generosity; it's an act of respect and trust.

are you worthy?

Ask yourself the following questions to see if you are likely to attract quality referrals:

- ❋ **Are you a positive, likable person? Do others enjoy working with you?**

- ❋ **Are you communicating to others in ways that will help them see that you are a good fit for the types of clients, projects, or opportunities you wish to attract?**

- ❋ **Do you have a track record that fosters respect and trust?**

- ❋ **Can others consistently rely on you to do good work, offer good service, meet deadlines, and create positive results?**

* **Would they trust you to capably and honorably serve a family member or their best friend, most profitable client, or most highly regarded colleague?**

* **If they refer or connect you to others, will the results make them look like a hero?**

If you can answer an unequivocal "yes" to these questions, you are likely to attract more of what you want in the way of referrals as you go about your business.

As we all know, the Golden Rule encourages us to treat others as we would want to be treated (or, to take it a step farther, as they would want to be treated). As this applies to attracting referrals, consider what you want from the people with whom you do business and to whom you'd consider making referrals. You expect good service and positive results without a lot of hassle or drama, right? You probably have a long list of other expectations as well.

try this!

Make a list of these traits and expectations that you want from others, both the people you do business with and the people you refer. Now turn these desires, expectations, and standards back on yourself. Are these standards and behaviors that you uphold and demonstrate in your work? If not, you have work to do. By far the best way to attract more customers and referrals is to give excellent service to the ones you already have.

Make your referral sources look like rock stars.

If someone is generous and trusting enough to send you a quality connection, lead, or referral, the first and best way to return the favor is by doing a superb job. Do all you can to make the person who sent something your way look good. If you do, the return on this investment will expand beyond your wildest imaginations. If you don't, expect the pipeline of referrals to dry up and quickly.

Express ample gratitude.

Remember, you are not entitled to referrals from others nor are they ever owed to you. It bears repeating that whenever someone shows you confidence by sending you a quality referral, lead, recommendation, opportunity, connection, introduction, or anything else of value, be sure to express ample gratitude. As old fashioned as it may sound, a sincere handwritten note sent by post is a simple, but classy way to stand above others who may only send a quick text message or email.

If a referral is not a fit, say no graciously.

I thought of a connection I wanted to make to a colleague who was seeking new business. I planned to introduce her to a colleague who had a business that complemented hers. My thinking was that they could potentially form a collaborative partnership. When I brought this up to my colleague, she graciously declined and told me she already had several long-standing colleagues with whom she was collaborating. She also shared with me some information that made it clear to me what she *was* looking for.

I appreciated and respected her immediate honesty and clarity on what she did and did not want. She actually has made it much easier for me to know and remember how I can help her and I respect her even more as a colleague and businesswoman. Had she not told me this, there could have been some awkward moments and wasted time and energy.

Let your people know in writing what you want.

Your people are probably hoping they can help you be successful. But don't make them guess what you need or how they can help. Know how to tactfully communicate your goals and needs clearly so others will know how they can be of service.

try this!

Carefully create and selectively distribute a one-page document that explains the services or products you currently offer and the ideal clients and opportunities you are seeking. This is not a long, detailed manifesto that you blast out in a mass mailing or dole out randomly at a networking event. Rather, it's a concise document you can present to your most trusted and valued friends, colleagues, clients, mentors, and other major supporters who want to help you and would appreciate knowing how.

Be direct, but use a tone of graciousness and humility. Keep the wording simple and free of complex jargon. Be informative, never sales-y. Make the document easy to scan and digest. Use lists and bullets if necessary. Express genuine interest in receiving a similar document from the recipient. Update and redistribute this document once a year or when you make major changes or shifts in your business.

Remember that many valuable referrals don't involve money or customers.

Many valuable referrals aren't technically referrals at all; they are connections, introductions, recommendations, or forms of feedback. These can include:

❊ **Opportunities for visibility, publicity, credibility, or recognition**

- Publicity opportunities
- Speaking engagements
- Nominations for awards or honors in your profession or community

❊ **Connections and introductions**

- Influential friends or colleagues
- Potential mentors

❊ **Groups to belong to or events and conferences to attend**

- Networking and business development groups
- Professional associations
- Small groups and mastermind gatherings
- Conferences, workshops, and other professional development events

❊ **Advice, information, resources, and feedback**

- Best practices and systems to try/implement
- Books, publications, articles, and blogs to read
- Podcasts to listen to
- Business, industry, or community news

❊ **Actions and corrections**

- Feedback on an aspect of your business
- A new product, service, vendor, or supplier to try

These non-monetary referrals can bring significant and immeasurable value to your business, so treat them with the same respect as any referral to a paying client or opportunity. Note how they pan out into paying opportunities and other forms of advancement for you and your business.

> Referrals, recommendations, and connections are precious gifts. They are a special type of currency that involves a lot of trust, clarity, and understanding. The good referrals and introductions take time and effort to cultivate and are the products of strong, solid, trusting relationships.

try this!

Collect testimonials and references when you've earned them. If you have happy customers, ask them graciously for a testimonial or a letter of reference soon after you've delivered the goods. These are "referral credits" because you are essentially asking for proof of someone's trust and endorsement of you and your business, that you can use in your promotional materials or on your website. As with any request for a referral, don't make the mistake of asking for a testimonial unless you are certain you've created excellent results, exceeded expectations, earned your clients' trust, and brought them consistent and noteworthy value.

To help my people with testimonials, I sometimes send them a short questionnaire asking for feedback. I ask four simple questions:

1. Why did you hire me?

2. What value did I bring to you or your organization?

3. What could I do better?

4. Is there anything else you'd like to tell me?

Then I pay attention to the answers, acting on areas where I can make improvements.

How does all this relate to being an Intentional Networker?

Attracting referrals is not about shamelessly inflicting yourself, your product, your services, or even your pitch onto anyone who will listen in the hopes of getting their attention, their business, their loyalty, or their endorsement. It is not about randomly pitching to others and asking them to "put the word out" or "tell your friends."

Attracting referrals involves a consistent and sincere investment in building relationships, creating consistently positive results, and earning unyielding trust. It requires you to pay attention to and practice as best you can the ideas, tips, and techniques you've read about in this book. Attracting rewarding relationships, respect, referrals, and results is about making every preparation possible, following through thoughtfully, and then creating an environment that's irresistible for attraction, priceless relationships, trust, loyalty, and growth.

why do this work?

If you've reached this page and have read everything contained in this book, you've perused literally hundreds of stories, ideas, tips, and suggestions on how to improve and develop yourself, your vision, your relationships, and your connection tactics and strategies. All this was included in this book for a reason: to help you become not only more focused, strategic, and intentional, but also more polished, memorable, connected, thoughtful, and trustworthy. And not just as a networker, but also as a business person, colleague, friend, and human being. These are the prerequisites for attracting referrals and results for your business. Practice what you've read here and there is no question you will stand out from the crowd and become more attractive in the best possible way.

In short, your referral quotient will shoot way up.

But, gosh, you might be saying, remembering, practicing, and mastering every suggestion, every tip, every bit of advice included in these pages seems so overwhelming and daunting, if not impossible! Sure, it might seem that way at first. That's okay. Take it a step at a time. Make a promise to yourself to implement something you've read here each day. Keep honing and practicing. As you do, something amazing will happen: you will change and evolve into *The Intentional Networker* you aspire to become.

Let this book serve as a field guide or manual you refer to when you need a surge of networking inspiration. Keep it handy for regular reference. Highlight sections that speak to you. Scribble in the margins. Dog ear the pages. Discuss sections with your colleagues or coaches. See what works best for you.

Here is one final note about why striving to become a more Intentional Networker is important. After being in business for myself for more than twenty years, observing and comparing notes with my most successful mentors and colleagues, and checking in with other business experts, the biggest reason to do the work outlined in this book is this: it actually works! It has worked for me and many others. I'm confident it can work for you, too.

resources & bibliography

Please visit www.intentionalnetworker.com/resources for a list of recommended books, blogs, websites, and other resources that can help you become a more Intentional Networker.

index

acknowledgments

Writing and publishing a book is not a project for the faint-hearted, nor is it a task that can be accomplished solo or over a weekend. How fitting, then, that this book is about attracting powerful relationships, referrals, and results in business. It serves as a concrete example of what you can accomplish when you know what you want, set clear intentions, and open up to discovering and developing solid relationships with the right people who can help.

There were many such people who showed up in my world at just the right time. They influenced my decision to write this book, supported me on the journey, and provided valuable resources, guidance, and expertise along the way.

First, I am filled with love and gratitude for my husband Paul and son Ryan who love and support me unconditionally; inspire me with their hard work, strength, and courage; share my desire to make a positive impact on others; and give me the freedom to be who I am and do what I want to do. Even our dog Maggie was patient and supportive, but knew exactly when to pester me to take her out for a refreshing, head-clearing walk.

I'm grateful to Sandra Yancey and the team at eWomenNetwork. The work they do, the network they have built, and the events they host allow entrepreneurial women like me to think and dream bigger and gain access to the experts and resources we need, when we need them. Sandra introduced me and many others to Mary Ann Halpin and her Fearless Women Movement in 2008. This in turn influenced my decision to move fearlessly forward with my dream of writing a book.

Special thanks and recognition also go to my publishing strategist, Jan B. King of the eWomenPublishingNetwork. Jan has been a reliable, generous, dedicated, and encouraging ally throughout the writing and publishing process. She kept me on track, focused, and energized, especially on the days when all I could see were pages filled with words and a To Do list four miles long. I wish I had recorded our many phone conversations as they were priceless!

I also send my love and gratitude to my friend and advisor, Dianna Amorde. She introduced me to Jan as she was on her own journey toward book publication. Dianna also was among those who agreed to review and critique my manuscript. Other reviewers included: BrandyAmstel, Kim Brill, Doug Hall, Korey Howell, Christine Moline, Cindy Niels, Leslie Roan, Sylvia Stern, and Darlene Templeton. Thanks to each of you for your time, honest comments, and valuable suggestions!

When it was time to pare and polish my manuscript and pay keen attention to details without losing sight of the big picture, Jan introduced me to Kim Pearson. Kim has been a fabulous editor and has become a great friend as well. Again, it's those quality relationships and referrals that serve as catalysts for more great relationships and results.

Other members of my book publishing team are my: author's assistant, Janica Smith; graphic designer, Bella Guzmán; photographer, Korey Howell; website specialist, Amy Hufford; proofreader Clarisa Marcee; indexer Nancy Humphreys; and my gifted chiropractor Dr. Tenesha Weine. Thank you for all you do for me.

Many other friends have routinely provided guidance, inspiration, honest feedback, stimulating conversation, fresh perspectives, or a well-timed phone call, cup of coffee, or glass of wine. Among these are: Cameron Babberney, Brenda Bailey, Monica Benoit-Beatty, Connie Brubaker, Sara Canaday, Jean Carpenter-Backus, Diane Carroll, Jim Comer, Jan Goss, Jill Griffin, Vikki Loving, Lorie Marrero, Keith Miller, Ricci Neer, the late Annie Durrum Robinson, Lynn "Lindy" Segall, Anne Tiedt, and Renée Trudeau.

Finally, I want to express my gratitude to the many clients and talent network members I've worked with over the years. You have helped me build my business and taught me many valuable lessons. Thanks also to the people within the professional organizations that inspire, educate, and energize me as a communicator and entrepreneur: The Association for Women Communications (AWC); the National Speakers Association (NSA), Texas Women in Business (TWIB), Wisdom at Work, and Marcia Wieder's Dream University. You have provided me with fertile ground for my professional development and for making and growing many powerful, rewarding relationships.

about the author

An award-winning connector and communicator, Patti DeNucci has studied, practiced, and taught the art and science of intentional networking and strategic referrals for more than twenty-five years.

After seven years as a marketing communications executive and twelve years as a freelance writer and consultant, Patti launched DeNucci & Co. LLC, a referral service firm, in 2001. Here Patti helps businesses and organizations connect strategically to the top-notch experts and resources they need to handle their projects and challenges. To date, her work with DeNucci & Co. represents millions of dollars in projects and connections.

An experienced speaker, Patti has presented, facilitated discussions, and emceed at numerous businesses, events, and conferences. She also has been quoted, interviewed, profiled, and published in numerous media, including: Fox, *Southwest Airlines Spirit Magazine*, *Working Mother*, *Austin Woman Magazine*, *Austin Business Journal*, *Austin American-Statesman*, and others.

Patti serves on the founding board of the new National Speakers Association (NSA) chapter in Austin, Texas and is founder of Freelance Austin, a networking and professional-development organization for business-minded freelancers, consultants, and solopreneurs. She also has held leadership positions for the Austin chapters of eWomenNetwork™ and the Association for Women in Communications and is a founding member of Impact Austin, a philanthropic organization that encourages women to pool their resources to give more than $500,000 in grants to worthy non-profits each year.

In 2008, Patti was selected as one of forty female entrepreneurs from across North America to be featured in Mary Ann Halpin's book *Fearless Women, Fearless Wisdom*. She is also a featured expert in *101 Great Ways to Enhance Your Career* by Michelle A. and David Riklan (SelfGrowth.com).

In recognition of her ongoing leadership and initiative, the Professional Chapter of the Association for Women in Communications chose Patti for both its Outstanding Chapter Member and Mentor Awards in the 1990s. She has also been nominated for AWC's Outstanding Austin Communicator and Creative Initiative Awards, the Austin Women's Chamber of Commerce Spirit of Women Award, Working Mother Magazine's Raising a Ruckus Award, and the Austin Business Journal's Profiles in Power Award.

Patti welcomes your comments and suggestions. You can reach her at:

EMAIL   patti@denucciandcompany.com

PHONE   512-418-0527

TWITTER   www.twitter.com/pattidenucci

Please visit **www.IntentionalNetworker.com** to sign up for Patti's newsletter and to receive additional tips, resources, and announcements on events and programs designed to help you network more intentionally so you can attract more powerful relationships, referrals, and results in business.

Spread the word (intentionally, of course!)

Interested in additional copies of *The Intentional Networker: Attracting Powerful Relationships, Referrals & Results in Business*?

Know others who could benefit from it?

We'd love to hear from you if you want:

⁂ **To order additional books**

⁂ **To learn about special discount pricing on 10 or more copies of the book**

⁂ **More information about Intentional Networker coaching, consulting, and strategic work sessions**

⁂ **To hire Patti DeNucci to speak at your event**

⁂ **To share an Intentional Networking story or tip**

⁂ **To offer feedback or comments on this book**

Voice: 512-418-0527
Fax: 512-418-0528
Email: info@intentionalnetworker.com

Mail:

Rosewall Press
A division of DeNucci & Co. LLC
5114 Balcones Woods Drive 307-430
Austin, TX 78759

www.facebook.com/TheIntentionalNetworker.com

www.intentionalnetworker.com

ORDER FORM

Use this convenient form to order additional copies of
*The Intentional Networker: Attracting Powerful Relationships,
Referrals & Results in Business*

Please send me ____ copies at $19.95 each   _____
(call for bulk order discounts)

Postage and handling – Add $4.95 per book _____

+ $3.00 each for each additional book   _____

Texas residents add 8.25% sales tax   _____

               Total _____

__Enclosed is my check (*payable to DeNucci & Co., LLC*)

__Please charge my credit card #_____

__ Visa _MasterCard ___ AmEx

_____exp date ___ three digit code on back

Signature_____

PLEASE PRINT

Name_____

Address_____

City_____ State_____ Zip _____

Phone ( ) _____-_____

Email _____

CPSIA information can be obtained at www.ICGtesting.com

234326LV00002B/2/P